C 63288

THE TIME DIARIES
of
JULIAN FANE

BY THE SAME AUTHOR

Morning
A Letter
Memoir in the Middle of the Journey
Gabriel Young
Tug-of-War
Hounds of Spring
Happy Endings
Revolution Island
Gentleman's Gentleman
Memories of My Mother
Rules of Life
Cautionary Tales for Women
Hope Cottage
Best Friends
Small Change
Eleanor
The Duchess of Castile
His Christmas Box
Money Matters
The Social Comedy
Evening
Tales of Love and War
Byron's Diary
The Stepmother
The Sodbury Crucifix
Damnation
Games of Chance

The Collected Works of Julian Fane
Volumes I, II, III, IV & V

The Harlequin Edition

Three Stories of Boyhood
Secrets of the Confessional
A Reader's Choice
A Writer's Life for Me
How to Publish Yourself
A Bad Experience
Mistress of Arts
Can Women Say No?
Ralph's Religion
How to be a Writer
Snobs
The Harrison Archive
In Short

THE TIME DIARIES
of
JULIAN FANE

Book Guild Publishing
Sussex, England

First published in Great Britain in 2005 by
The Book Guild Ltd
25 High Street
Lewes, East Sussex
BN7 2LU

Copyright © Julian Fane 2005

The right of Julian Fane to be identified as the author of this work has been asserted by him in accordance with the Copyright, Designs and Patents Act 1988.

All rights reserved. No part of this publication may be reproduced, transmitted, or stored in a retrieval system, in any form or by any means, without permission in writing from the publisher, nor be otherwise circulated in any form of binding or cover other than that in which it is published and without a similar condition being imposed on the subsequent purchaser.

The two paragraphs offering advice on 'How to Grow Old Gracefully' have already appeared in the anthology *Late Youth*, edited by Suzanna Johnston and published by Acadia Books.

Typesetting in Garamond by
Keyboard Services, Luton, Bedfordshire

Printed in Great Britain by
Antony Rowe Ltd, Chippenham, Wiltshire

A catalogue record for this book is available from
The British Library

ISBN 1 85776 945 7

To
G

Contents

Marking Time	1
Extra Time	83
Time Scale	207
Index	213

MARKING TIME

It might be thought that, owing to my age, the title of Part One of these diaries is synonymous with the modern catch phrase 'Waiting for God'. Not so – marking time is part of our military vocabulary and describes marching on the spot, preparatory as a rule to receiving the order 'Forward march!'

1999

11 June 1999

Patsy Grigg, wife of John, wrote me a letter appreciative of *Evening*, but saying she was worried by the final paragraph of the book. *Evening* has just been published, and balances my first book, *Morning*, published nearly fifty years ago. I end the story of *Evening* by announcing that it is my last puppet show, my adieu to fiction, at least in principle.

12 June

It is the next day; and, like all authors, I have more to say – and to say on the same subject. I cannot retire, authors don't, authors won't – I would be ill if I did, or under ground. What then am I to write? The answer seems to be this diary. My approach to the undertaking is diffident. I have never before kept a diary, and feel I do not belong to the strange tribe of diarists. I have never begun a book that has no end in view.

But there is really no alternative. Notwithstanding my lucky facility in respect of plots, stories, inventions, I am not sure that I could produce another novel which was new.

Questions touching my diary remain. The brave modern answer would probably be: 'Go for it!'

13 June

My half-sister June was named after the month of her birth. Our mother was married and widowed three times before she was fifty-six. By her second husband, Arthur Capel, she had two daughters, Anne [Higgins] and June. June married first the distinguished pianist Franz Osborn, and produced her only child Christopher, and after Franz's premature death married Jeremy Hutchinson, Queen's Counsel and now peer of the realm.

Yesterday afternoon G and I went to have tea with the Hutchinsons in their home in the Sussex Downs. June for the moment is well, and in her brave way has thrown off memories of her lifelong battle against ill health, and Jeremy looks twenty years younger than his age. Their hospitality is exemplary – and I am the most objective of guests. Their welcome could hardly be warmer, they concentrate on you for all they are worth, listen to you without interrupting, allow general conversation, steer clear of controversy, and do their utmost to feed you well and make you comfortable. June supported my bid to become a writer – from my schooldays onwards – when others were against it. She bought the house in London where I lived for nearly two decades, and without which I would have had no settled address.

14 June

Spoke to Patsy Grigg on the telephone yesterday. She explained to me that the last page of *Evening* worried her not because it was incomprehensible, but because it seemed to signal my decision to write or to publish no more books, fiction in particular. I thanked her for the compliment, and said, 'Well, perhaps and maybe'.

But I have not yet changed my mind. The distance increases between me and Grub Street, where rats race and backs are bitten, and I note the receding prospect with complacence.

Also, yesterday, the first night of the revived production of Handel's *Rodelinda* at Glyndebourne. G loved every minute, I enjoyed it, and the audience applauded loud and long. But I am not a critic, except of unqualified journalists who air destructive views of the life-work of artists in newspapers.

16 June

Tonight is G's big night at Glyndebourne. She has free use of the Glyndebourne Box and its ten seats: that is her annual reward for being a director of the main Glyndebourne board. She is the longest-serving director apart from George Christie himself, and only the second female director ever since George's father and mother, John and Audrey Christie, founded the opera house in 1934. G is due to retire at the end of this year and before the next millennium begins. She may be sad to call it a day; but all she cares about in this context is the good of Glyndebourne and the art of opera.

18 June

In the night, just as we were dropping off to sleep, our dog Meg began to bark under our spare room with a couple of guests in it. Meg is over a hundred in human terms if her age is multiplied by seven, and goes in for long spells of irritable spaced-out barking, whether for the sake of food or to attract attention or for other reasons. We told her to shut up; let her out into the garden, although she is accustomed to make messes in the kennel if taken short; we scolded, threatened, attempted to bribe her – all in vain. She stopped until we were back in bed, then began again. The tailpiece to the story – no pun intended – is that our guests vowed at breakfast that they had not heard a single bark during the night: could it be true?

I have revised the TSS of the last two of my fifteen little books in the Harlequin Edition, *The Harrison Archive*, descriptive of the schizophrenia of the twentieth century, its humanity and its barbarism, and *In Short*, my tribute to Ursula Codrington, who lived for art and typed for me for some years.

19 June

Saturday morning, and for me business as usual. My routine of work for half a century has been five hours of writing or trying to write until one p.m. for seven days a week. That makes only thirty-five hours of writing weekly, not much in comparison with Tolstoy's boast that he sometimes wrote for twelve hours at a stretch, and not a great deal relative to the average forty-eight or forty hour working week.

But William Douglas-Home, the playwright,

advised me when I was nineteen or twenty that I had better learn to sleep at any old hour of the day or night, since writers can only get away from their work by sleeping.

20 June

Tony Shephard has recently moved into the basement flat of the house next to ours, and we were told he was keen to meet us. Had he read my books, I wondered, as authors will. Eventually we were introduced and he invited us in for a drink and a great surprise. He has turned his flat into a mini-museum dedicated – consecrated almost – to the upper crust. Life-size cut-outs of Queen Victoria and other royal ladies have been padded, robed, bejewelled and crowned. Crowns and coronets are everywhere. Chairs bear the royal insignia, and have been sat on by peers and peeresses at functions. There are pictures of royalty, books about royal personages, family trees, menus of royal repasts. Tony guided us from treasure to treasure with charm and expertise. And he dealt diplomatically with his special interest in me. He had a complete list of everybody in Westminster Abbey for the coronation of King George VI in 1937, and my name was included as Page to the Marquess of Cholmondeley.

Tony was born and brought up in the East End; gravitated to Sussex; has spent his life, and is spending his retirement, in looking after people; and mounts exhibitions of his royal collection to raise money for charities.

* * *

What are these: The Chinese Character, The Common Pug, The Sallow Kitten, The Dingy Footman, The White Ermine, The True Lover's Knot, The Clouded Drab, The Snout? Answer is caterpillars.

21 June

My friend Carlo, the playwright and translator Carlo Ardito, a recent convert to the Internet, is not so interested as he used to be in our domestic politics. Our country is becoming a cipher, he tells me. Great Britain or England or whatever we are now meant to call it is not even mentioned by the international media as participating with the USA in the bombing of Kosovo.

23 June

Politics for me is like cheerfulness was for Oliver Edwards – it keeps breaking in (see Boswell's *Johnson*).

John Grigg wrote to me yesterday about *Evening*. He is not only a historian, but a literary man in the old-fashioned, widest and most admirable sense. He pays me a compliment in urging me not to regard *Evening* as my last book; but has discovered it is what he calls a 'tract', and says he has a prejudice against 'tracts'.

I am afraid I have done it before – there always seems to have been a 'tract' in me struggling to get out. And I like 'tracts' as much as John dislikes them: I like an author to generalise, to illustrate a truth or a truism, and always to have morality or a moral in mind. *Evening* has the humblest of links with Plato's *Symposium*. It was meant to be the summing-up of my experience of the grades of love. I respect John so much that I can see his point and differ from him without difficulty.

24 June

Sir David Frost OBE merits congratulations. He first made his mark as a guerrilla satirist in the class war, but now he himself is an internationally respected member of the Establishment. Can it be true that he too is heading for that Eldorado of entertainment, crime? There is a rumour going round that he is a backer of a film about Nick Leeson, who betrayed the trust of his employers, defrauded and broke Barings Bank, and ruined innumerable lives. The film, good or bad, will make Leeson into a hero or anti-hero, and rub salt into the wounds of his innocent victims. I expect the scurrilous rumour is unfounded. We have all hoped Sir David had become the sort of knight who is *sans reproche*.

25 June

People of my age are surprised and not necessarily displeased when I ask them about their medication – in layman's lingo, what pills they take. They are apt to bridle and reply that the subject is boring, that polite people are supposed not to show the scars of their operations, and the less said the better. But I am pleased to inform them: 'At last we have something of mutual interest to talk about.'

Today I am giving away the hefty volume entitled: Debrett's *Distinguished People of Today 1990*. I have replaced it with a 'classless' edition of the same work entitled: *People of Today 1999*.

26 June

I note, and almost begin to enjoy, the relaxation of discipline in writing a diary in comparison with the writing of my kind of books.

A strong socialist wins the Lottery – what does he do with five million pounds, what do five million pounds do to him? He could have a wife whom he adores – she could have bought the Lottery ticket. He could have a daughter with expensive tastes. Subject of the story: the contradiction between socialism and human nature, or, to put it another way, between the idealism and the corruption responsible for the hypocrisy that has ruled in my lifetime.

Do-gooders live in another world, where realism is out of order. In my hearing a friend of ours told liberal-minded X that he and his neighbours were scared of a local criminal, a convicted car thief, mugger, burglar, who is large, strong, probably mad, and threatens everybody when he is out of prison that he is planning to break and enter their houses; to which X commented sympathetically, referring to the criminal, 'Poor chap!' Yet X fights like a tiger for his own and his wife's privileged way of life, and I cannot believe he would like it if he and his family in their first, second or third homes were burgled and beaten up.

A do-gooder is a person who attempts to please somebody (singular or plural) at somebody else's expense.

27 June

Is it a new horror or an old one? I used to think that the upper classes and people in authority were stereotyped by popular entertainers, and denigrated as morons and buffoons, owing to ignorance. But I have recently come to suspect that they are not mocked for fun, not in the P G Wodehouse manner or in music-hall terms, but in a politically motivated attempt to rob toffs and bosses of their humanity and turn them into objects fit to be hated, like the stuffed dummies we were trained to bayonet in the army. The Russian communists did the same thing to the kulaks before liquidating them, and the nazis did it to the Jews.

Spoke to Ben Glazebrook, Chairman of Constable, my publisher and friend, yesterday afternoon. He rang me and apologised for having been hard to reach for the last fortnight – he has been in

Paris and America. He said he had had enough of life in the fast lane, and longed only to crawl along in the slowest of all possible lanes.

30 June

If I knew more, was learned, a historian, and had time to burn, I would write a book entitled *Second Sons*. I believe they are an interesting class of person in countries where primogeniture is more or less in force in the top families – that is, the principle of the first-born son's entitlement to the lion's share of family treasure.

Primogeniture is a good idea, in fact essential in order to conserve the social fabric, especially when an inheritance includes a title, a stately home and a great estate. The alternative is some sort of division of the spoils between the children, probably the end of the family home, the break-up of the estate, and disputes and litigation.

Primogeniture however, for all its advantages, can raise awkward questions. What happens if his lordship happens to sire male twins? The twin who politely ushers his brother into the light of day and follows a few minutes later may be renouncing a fortune. What if the twins are identical – it would seem to aggravate the injustice – and what if they are delivered by Caesarean section? – the surgeon in charge could be enriching one and impoverishing the other.

Exemplars of the good or the bad luck of second sons abound. King George V obtained both the regal destiny of his deceased elder brother and his brother's fiancée, Princess Mary of Teck.

George VI was a second son, enthroned thanks to Wallis Simpson, who rid us all of Edward VIII. The late John Wyndham, 6th Lord Leconfield of Petworth and 1st Lord Egremont, and two dukes, Devonshire* and Beaufort, were raised to the seats of power when their brothers were killed in the 1939–1945 war: what were and are their thoughts on the subject of fate?

I donate the above to whoever is able to mine this seam of drama and perhaps of gold.

1 July

Last night at the Final Rehearsal of Puccini's *Manon Lescaut*. The Romanian Adina Nitescu sang Manon, as she did in the original production two years ago; but she has become beautiful in the interval, a beautiful actress and a lovely singer.

2 July

Harriet Bridgeman, of Bridgeman Art Library fame, and more to the point our friend, wrote me a postcard that includes the gratifying sentence: 'I heard [my mother speaking] of the rare excellence of the modern morality story she was reading.' The morality story was *Evening*, which is a tract to John Grigg.

We were speaking of the difficulty some men have in extricating themselves from the arms of some women, and, of course, vice versa. Franz

---

*Andrew, 12th Duke of, deceased.

Liszt, pianist, composer, irresistible magnet for the opposite sex, and eventually Abbé, did it with wit and charm according to the following anecdote. He spent the night with his mistress of the moment at the hotel where she was staying, then walked out on her. In the morning the lady – to give her the benefit of the doubt – discovered she had been abandoned and created a tremendous scene, breaking everything she could lay hands on. Later in the day she prepared to depart and to pay the bill for her room. The manager of the hotel informed her that the gentleman had paid for it. She then offered to pay for breakages, the crockery, mirror, vase for flowers and picture frames she had smashed. The manager said that the gentleman had left enough money to pay for breakages too.

4 July

Yesterday evening, the first public performance of the revival of *Manon Lescaut* at Glyndebourne. Apparently the star of the show, Nitescu, said at midday that she was too ill to sing; at 2 p.m. she said she might sing; George Christie talked to her and at 6.15 p.m. she did sing – she sang marvellously throughout and was cheered to the echo.

A well-known, not to say notorious, opera critic refused Glyndebourne's invitation to be present, and therefore, like most critics, failed to give great art its due.

Pat Gibson there, we met him in the garden and

talked briefly. He said how happy he was to be eighty-three – he needs to do no more fundraising. He has had a brilliant career, ending up a lord covered in honours of one sort and another. Pat and Dione Gibson are or could be our friends if my reclusive and their gregarious tendencies could ever bring about meetings. Dione's sister Lavinia Smiley, whom I never knew, once wrote to me to say a book of mine had saved her life, a claim which unfortunately proved not to be true.

6 July

I had lunch with Ben Glazebrook yesterday. He greeted me with the news that Constable has lost a contract bringing in a large part of its annual earnings. As a result, he is going to have to reorganise the company, reduce his shareholding, change his life. He was nonetheless philosophical, could see silver linings to the gathering clouds, and without delay switched the conversation to talking about my interests. He urged the publication of the remaining two volumes of my *Collected Works* – making five in all – in this financial year, before the fifth of April 2000, instead of gradually over the next two years. He wished the whole *Collected Works* might be published under his – the Constable – imprint. I was and am in full agreement.

Should I have been, should I be, more worried?

No recluse has ever entertained more guests than me.

8 July

G has taken our dogs to be stripped of their excessive coats for summer wear. Handling four Cairn Terriers in busy Cliffe High Street after finding somewhere to park her car proves her love of dogs in general and ours in particular.

The BBC is putting on a documentary about life and death in communist Russia. It will show that communism in that country, that country alone, tortured to death ten or eleven times as many people as nazism did likewise to Jews and others. Whereas the BBC has been publicising the sins of nazism and the suffering of the Jews for a good half-century, this programme will surely be its first attempt to draw popular attention to the much more heinous sins and crimes of communism, marxism, extreme socialism and the rabid left in power. Why the silence? Answer: the truth has been systematically censored by our homegrown lefties, who still want to turn England red, blood red. Even my books and stories that refer to the horrific record of marxism/socialism have been reviled by critics who cling to their quaint faith in the godliness of Karl Marx and the marxist 'opium of the people'.

10 July

I have been preparing six of my books for reissue, three in volume IV of my *Collected Works* and three more in Volume V, the final one, so as to have them ready for Ben to publish at short notice if he is to lose his Constable imprint. But I only correct the howlers and the misprints that have weighed on my conscience. I cannot put myself in the various shoes I was wearing when I wrote the books: other writers have not done themselves much good with their belated second thoughts.

Our Prime Minister now threatens to imprison anyone who kills a fox, while he pardons and lets out of prison the IRA's killers of human beings.

11 July

Watched one and a quarter hours of the three hour docudrama *Gulag*, screened last night by the BBC. All the blame for all the casualties of the Russian communist Terror is put on Stalin. This must be to mollify the worshippers of Marx and Lenin, who were at least as, and arguably more, responsible. The bodies of the many millions of victims of the Terror were hidden, so the communists knew they were doing wrong.

12 July

Watched the rest of *Gulag*. Both true and moving, the final statement of the woman of Norilsk in Siberia: 'All our suffering was for nothing.'

Gulag, the TV programme, reminds me of Dieter Tressler. Regrettably, I have never used the autobiographical papers he gave me. But my memory is still fairly reliable, and brevity may be tactful – there have been so many books about terrible individual fates. Is Dieter dead or alive? None of us knows. If the latter, I send him congratulations and love from all the surviving members of my family.

13 July

Dieter's War: my half-sisters Anne and June met him in Austria in the late thirties. He was the son of a famous Austrian actor called Tressler, and was a gentle, fey, romantic and athletic youth. He loved flying and was proud of his pilot's licence. He fell in love with a girl in my sisters' party and dropped red roses on her from an aeroplane.

My sisters invited him to stay at Lyegrove, our home, and he spent ten days or a fortnight with us in the summer of 1937 and again in 1938. He yodelled; he could lift my three sisters, my brother and me simultaneously; he made us a marvellous house in a tree; he climbed a drainpipe and did acrobatics at the top; and in the disused quarry where we swam in spring water he dived off a towering cliff. No wonder we all loved him.

After the war he told me what happened next. The nazis called him up into the Luftwaffe; but he was not prepared to drop bombs on his English friends and decided to seek asylum in Switzerland. He deserted his post, a capital offence, and fled Germany by way of the high mountains at night.

All went well until he either missed his footing in the dark or was caught in an avalanche, tumbled downhill and lost consciousness. When he came to he was nearer the Swiss border than he expected to be, only about five yards from it, but he had broken bones, he could not move although he could hear the guards and their dogs, and was duly arrested and condemned to death.

His parents got to know of his plight. They were acquainted with Frau Goering, Emmy Goering, and appealed to her to use her influence in order to save Dieter's life. They were successful up to a point. His sentence was commuted, instead of facing the firing squad he was enrolled in the company of real and so-called criminals who were forced to walk across minefields ahead of the German army. He survived to be captured by the Russians and sentenced to fifteen years in the Siberian concentration camps.

Again, somehow, he survived, returned to Austria and in time contacted my sister Anne. I met him in her house in the sixties and he spoke about his experiences. He was recognisable, his fine physique had served him well, but he said his digestion was ruined by starvation and rotten food. He had done better than most of the other victims of communist justice because he could play tunes on a home-made whistle and draw portraits of his gaolers. He had also won favours by helping to stack the stiffly frozen corpses of his companions as if they had been lengths of wood – they were chucked into mass graves when the weather allowed.

In comparison with the pre-war Dieter with his Viennese temperament, fun-loving, sentimental, irrepressible and charming, he seemed a broken man. He had become a sort of mystic and perhaps a seer – part of him was withdrawn and out of reach. The changes in him were not only understandable, but surprisingly minor in view of all he had been through.

The last we heard of or from him, news he communicated to my sister June, was that he had married a woman much younger than he was.

15 July

Off to Chichester to see Jonathan Cecil acting the part of the Reverend Canon Chasuble in *The Importance of Being Earnest*.

16 July

Jonathan has mastered the art of projecting his own eccentricity. He is now as funny on stage as he always was off it.

17 July

Being my age is like fighting in the trenches in the 1914 war. Friends 'catch one' in the performance of their duties, friends who put their heads above the parapet are 'asking for it', friends are constantly getting wounded and stretchered back to a casualty station, or are shell-shocked by all the bad news and turn into nervous wrecks or take to drink, or fall down and die almost as one is talking to them.

I suppose I should be impervious by now, especially because so many of my friends were older than me. Often it was my books that made friends of us. And how flattering it was to be on friendly terms with them, particularly with the writers and artists, and to be able to turn to them for guidance! The other side of the medal was that I lost them too soon, too soon from my point of view, and sometimes feel I have been in mourning for most of my life.

I had written *Morning* by the time I was in my mid-twenties, and Arthur Koestler thought I was too young to rush into print. I protested that I was not rushing, having been writing full-time and flat out for six or seven years. Belatedly I see his point – I knew nothing of the darker side of life. Yet the books of youth have a quality that age cannot supply.

How brave our ill friends are!

18 July

Another hot blue morning. It is already eleven o'clock and I have done no literary work to speak of – what a change! I used to feel guilty and/or resentful to lose or be robbed of five minutes of my daily five hours of writing.

I have a hankering to tell a love story – a long-short story without cynicism.

Marina Picasso states in an interview that her

grandfather Pablo was a hateful monster who wreaked havoc on his rich and miserable extended family. And the other day some know-all told G that Evelyn Waugh died of disappointment, because he thought no one liked his books. Two unsurprising stories!

20 July

Our friend Judy Brittain staying, and going with G to *Rodelinda* this evening. We discussed the Don Juans of our acquaintance, a subject of unfailing interest. She said so cleverly that they fall into two categories: flash mice or flash rats. But I have known Don Juans who were not at all flash. One was a middle-aged stage manager with greying wiry hair and a misleadingly desiccated appearance – he was not rich, handsome, young or smart, but either he said, or others said it, that he never took a ride on a bus without stepping off with a woman in tow. Another Don Juan I know is so small that he must creep into the beds of women without their really knowing he is there and what he is doing to them – I suppose he would be a flash mouse, though not noticeably flashy. All that is certain in this field of study is that men can and do fail to spot the Don Juans in their midst. Tall, dark and handsome may not win the prize – think of all the beauties with their hideous lovers and husbands!

21 July

How did I ever have time to write proper books?

22 July

Not long ago I wrote an essay which I hoped would make another Harlequin book. It was about society, High Society or what is believed in some quarters to be the Society that is High. But the subject was like quicksand – I sank whichever way I turned. The truth is that, although there is a sort of High Society which is secret, exclusive, almost indefinable but certainly indestructible, there are many other societies, cliques, clubs, associations and so on, regarded as the highest of the high by those who yearn to be ushered through the relevant portals and by those already seated at the top tables.

Discreet people never discuss their nearest and dearest publicly. Nevertheless I feel compelled to record that G retired from the Board of Directors of Glyndebourne Productions Ltd yesterday, after serving for thirty-two years, during which period the original level of excellence of its productions has been maintained, and the beloved but rickety old opera house was replaced by the splendid and immediately beloved new one.

23 July

Following on from the above, yesterday we were at the dress rehearsal of Smetana's *The Bartered Bride*, a new production. Glyndebourne has succeeded in making an evening of delights out of an opera that can be as dull as ditchwater.

29 July

Where have the intervening days gone?

Another of my unfulfilled ambitions was to make a collection of comparisons such as 'dull as ditchwater', which have become part of the vernacular. One that I particularly like might be peculiar to Gloucestershire, where I was brought up and first heard it: 'as easy as feeding strawberries to a donkey'. They are apt to have hidden depths. In *Morning* I used the following, 'as easy as falling off a log'. The lady who translated the book into French never understood the ambiguity of the English and I failed to explain it either to her or to my own satisfaction. But now to try again: it is easy to fall off a log, indeed difficult not to fall off, but the fall may land you in a far from easy predicament, hurt you, break a bone, cripple you. The 'easy' meaning is encapsulated within a cautionary tale – the phrase warns that what is easy is not necessarily safe.

31 July

The wives of philanderers find contentment in having their husbands confined to quarters by illness and at last under their thumbs.

Chimney Sweeps, Gardeners' Garters, God's Grace, Mousetail, Smuts, Yorkshire Fog – what are they? Varieties of herbage.

2 August

A modern tragedy, which is as old as the hills: two young people fall in love. She is a strictly brought up virgin who works as a receptionist at an auction house. He is older, not a virgin, a smooth-talking salesman in a smart antique shop. They want each other badly – and she half-believes that sex is now the done thing, while he mumbles persuasive vows and undertakings. They are preoccupied by their sexual communings and experiments – she can think of nothing else. They cross another Rubicon by living together. But after a few months she realises that they have bypassed the authorisation of their love in church. She does not like to mention it, she shrinks from proposing marriage, she waits and hopes, but he says nothing, and she is embarrassed by the tentative inquiries of her family and the advice of her friends. It strikes her that she has given and is giving him her all, and that he has no reason to put the desired ring on her finger and assume a thousand new responsibilities. She loves him too much to leave him, and dare not cease to render any of her services in case he leaves her. She sleeps with and housekeeps for him without joy. She tells him she longs to have a child or children, but instead of taking the hint he groans with horror.

How does it end? She is bound to suggest marriage, and probably to nag him about it. He will then have reason to say they are too unhappy to tie a permanent knot. Her child-bearing years may be running out, his guilt may exacerbate the issue. He is more than likely to run away and marry a girl who has not become his mistress.

The moral of the story is that love is fated unless it is a fair do.

I am sorry to say that the harvest of all my experience, a generalisation proved by few exceptions, is that the twin forces that rule the world are not love and justice, but almost the reverse of those concepts, namely brute force and charm.

5 August

Off to Seaview, IOW, tomorrow for our week-long break. G's aunt had a house there and G's family was invited to stay in summer. She has fond memories of the place, and we have returned to the Seaview Hotel for this week in August for at least ten years. We hope to have the same room and usually get it. We can see and hear the sea fifty yards away at high tide. We walk and watch the dinghy races. At night we are lulled to sleep – with luck – by other holidaymakers eating and drinking and chatting and laughing in the hotel forecourt just below us. Everybody seems to be happy at Seaview.

Anne Higgins stayed with us for two nights and yesterday went to stay with her younger sister June Hutchinson. Anne is eighty. She lives in Marbella, Spain. Last year she fell ill and teetered on the edge of the next world. But she revived, and believes she has been granted a new lease of life by a chic London allergist. Quacks do a good job so long as they inspire confidence.

14 August

Home, home, not on the range, but where complications await.

Read Saul Bellow's *Herzog* on holiday: the whingeing overdone and the brilliance compromised by the showing-off. My best memory of *Herzog* is the following, which with apologies I quote without looking it up in the book: 'The most dangerous people are our leaders.'

15 August

At Seaview, laughing children and kind mothers and fathers made me think of the hearts and lives broken by divorce. Marriage should be made much more attractive financially to contract into, and much more expensive for both parties to contract out of. Women who marry for short-term gain, to wit the alimony, should be penalised, and the state should not subsidise single parenthood. Nothing changes minds and fashions so fast as pleasure or pain in the region of the wallet.

17 August

Sad for Anne Tree, as Michael grows iller daily. Her approach to the prospects and practicalities is selfless, positive and valiant.

18 August

Yesterday's hour-long programme on Channel 4 about the death of Michael Hutchence, a pop singer and the husband or lover of a media person called Paula Yates, was a fascinating insight into the immorality, amorality, perverseness, illogic, and crazed muddle that sections of the media promote nowadays. Hutchence in a hotel room in Australia spent the night drinking wines, spirits and cocktails, took cocaine, Prozac and Valium, and died of masturbating with the aid of asphyxia induced by his belt. The Australian coroner brought in a verdict of suicide, to which Yates was objecting. After revealing the lurid facts of her sex life with Hutchence, which sounded uncommonly like boasting, she explained that for the sake of herself and his child she wished the verdict had not been the discreet one of suicide but the squalid truth of death by wanking with trimmings under the influence of alcohol and legal and illegal drugs.

I have recovered from our holiday.

19 August

Ben Glazebrook and Constable have lost a considerable proportion of their business: what happens next? Ben has invited me to lunch in London to discuss the situation. If he manages to bring out the last two volumes of my *Collected Works*, I will be happy, and I believe that he with his characteristic generosity and integrity will be relieved. But we may end up with three vols of a five-vol edition.

20 August

A beautiful morning, blue sky with a few thin clouds looking like torn-off scraps of cotton wool, warm summery sunshine but autumnal in the shade, and all the people and the flies coming out to play.

21 August

I think more creatively in bed and half-asleep than at other times. I am most likely to solve problems in my work when I am shaving, like the writer Q (Sir Arthur Quiller-Couch). Recent rather unpleasant awakenings could be due to my not writing fiction and not 'living' two lives. In *Evening* I said goodbye to life in the never-never land of fiction. Maybe I was wrong. But a wrong can be righted. There is no law against changes of mind.

22 August

To London tomorrow to give lunch to Richard Tomkins and Miles Huddleston.

24 August

Lunch yesterday was gratifying as well as interesting. Richard told me the second printing of *Evening* was almost sold out. Miles is preparing a biography of James Stern, Jimmy Stern, short story writer and sometime powerful book critic in New York, and has just finished reading thirty years of J's diary, in which he found a mention of me. It refers to the night I spent with the Sterns at Hatch House, Tisbury, Wilts. The visit was no fun: Jimmy got drunk and never stopped nagging Tanya (how did she spell her name?). In the morning after the night before, he eventually emerged from his study to show me a drawing of his 'best friend', the late Brian Howard, notorious homosexual, which made my blood run rather cold. I left with the impression that I was not very welcome, although Jimmy had made more and more of an issue of my not coming down to see and stay with him. Our friendship went from high to low, in that it began with his wonderful letter out of the blue about my *Memoir in the Middle of the Journey*, and ended with the rudest of his increasingly rude letters and my reply that I could no longer continue our correspondence. Why exactly he was cross with me I never knew. He bullied me about not socialising with him more often, but perhaps it was love that he longed for in vain. He suffered from decades of writer's block, and was terribly embittered.

Tanya Stern was German, and before her marriage a physiotherapist in Berlin. Jimmy Stern's father, on being told of his son's matrimonial plans, employed a detective to investigate the fiancée. The detective reported that she was young and pretty and was visited by different men for approximately thirty minutes apiece on every day.

* * *

Will *Evening* be reprinted again, that is the question. The injustice of the bookshops' right to sell or return books will no doubt muck up our decision. To my knowledge a publisher stopped selling to a chainstore that used to order large quantities of new books and, when the publisher had invested in second printings, would return all the copies it had ordered still in unopened cartons.

27 August

Michael Tree died. He was a gifted draughtsman and painter and an extremely generous man. I only knew him well enough to know there was more to him than I knew. How will Anne manage? She has always lived in a family circle. But I think she will do well as a widow.

Richard Tomkins, self-styled Works Manager, that is to say the Director of Production at Constable who is responsible for my *Collected Works*, has lent me his copy of *The Children of the Sun* by Maurice Green. I have read one third. The author's subject, in modern jargon the literary glitterati of the twenties and thirties, is amusing; but his method is discouraging for readers. He begins by wading into a quagmire of analysis. His divisions of his 'children' into metaphorical fathers, sons and uncles, into dandies, naifs, Harlequins, Columbines and Pierrots, hunters and rogues, end in confusion worse confounded by innumerable qualifications – so-and-so is a

Harlequin but also a naif with a bit of rogue thrown in and a touch of uncle. I skipped as quickly as I could. But when Green gets down to thumbnail sketches and biographies he is good.

28 August

The Children of the Sun should be called *The Children of the Sewer*. Maurice Green's originals, liberating influences, coruscating talents, dominant personalities, could more accurately be described in the plural of a single inclusive word of four letters. He confirms me in my dim view of writers in general. I hero-worshipped them once upon a time. I stretched every sort of point to forgive Tolstoy his abominable behaviour in his older age. I was merely startled by Dostoevsky losing every penny of family funds by gambling, then beseeching his wife to give him her wedding ring to gamble with. I made allowances for Dickens' harsh treatment of Mrs Dickens, and Hardy for seldom speaking to the second Mrs Hardy, and a large percentage of all writers for their neuroses, psychoses, peccadillos, misdemeanours and offences. Success spoils almost everyone, and literary success seems to be especially reserved for people ready to stop at nothing. Maurice Green's book would justify, if I needed justification, my running a mile from Grub Street and its denizens

29 August

Those 'children of the sun' were mostly middle

class, middle-middle class. Their fathers were publishers or editors or journalists or hack writers, and they were often related, if distantly. A lot of their behaviour was cousinly competition, or sick sibling rivalry. They were snobs and social climbers, and ready to make exhibitions of themselves. They wanted to do better than their dim conventional fathers, while sticking roughly to the paternal lines of work. They also leant to the left. They tried to have it both ways with their capitalist tastes and their communist sympathies. No notice was taken of the crimes against humanity, already bad enough to make normal blood boil or run cold, committed in the USSR.

30 August

Yesterday evening at Glyndebourne was for me and surely many others perhaps the most memorable of countless memorable occasions. First we had the exquisite playing of *The Bartered Bride* overture by the LPO conducted by Jiri Kout, then the performance in the production by Nikolaus Lehnhoff, who must be the best opera producer in the world. It was the last night of the Festival, the audience was as usual well-disposed, recognised a good thing when they heard and saw it, and demanded curtain calls galore. Eventually the curtain rose on an empty stage and Gus Christie, George's second son, who is about to take over the Chairmanship of the opera house, walked on and gave an account of next year's programme. His nervousness did not show, his few words that were not informative were well-chosen, his easy warm yet strong personality came across the footlights, his handsome appearance combined with modesty no doubt had an effect, and he was given a rousing reception by the audience. Gus stepped aside and George entered, composed as ever despite the strain of his devotion to his duties. He spoke with characteristic wit and kept on saying how lucky he had been; but we all know he has made his luck by his own vision, drive, high-class standards, stubbornness and hard work. He was given a prolonged standing ovation, our friend Helen McCarthy, the stage manager, did not bring the curtain down, we all sang *For he's a jolly good fellow*, and the orchestra struck up The Queen according to the Glyndebourne tradition. Men and women of good will and good sense were thanking George and Mary and their family for having kept the flag of excellence and style flying for forty-odd years.

7 September

On 24 August, a fortnight ago, I stopped taking cortisone for polymyalgia, having tapered my dosage almost to nil on doctor's orders. No ill effects, and I feel far better, having lost about half or three quarters of a stone in weight – the false weight, or 'cushion effect', that cortisone is infamous for.

9 September

Lunched yesterday with Mark Bence-Jones at Brooks's. He has written good books – I especially admire *The Twilight of the Ascendancy* – and has been more than kind about mine. He is a generous host, and so learned that he cannot hear a surname without assuming it is linked to some historical event, noble lineage, ancient family, stately home, large estate.

Sentimental politicians of all persuasions have been wailing and gnashing their teeth, if they have any, over the death of Alan Clark, a dreadful man who mocked and sneered at them, and made nothing but mischief.

11 September

High-brow writers who publish porn under pseudonyms are really low-brow. High-class people cannot do low-class things: by acting common and being selfish and impolite you establish your true level. If you do not grace the top drawer, where you tell us you belong, you are fit only for the bottom drawer, the one beneath that which is reserved for the masses, who are not so pretentious.

Martin and Mish Dunne have been staying – a treat for us. They love their dogs almost as much as G loves ours – no one could love them more than she does. Some members of G's family going back for generations have been, and some still are, dog-crazy. But dog-crazy people love the human race too, and are more lovable than dog-haters.

15 September

I was invited to lunch at the Ritz Hotel yesterday. At the table next to ours sat Lady Jay of Paddington, Leader of the Labour Party in the House of Lords, with some young guests – her children by Peter Jay? She was attired in red, no doubt indicating her political inclination, looked very smart, and she and her party drank champagne. I was glad to see that yet another socialist appreciates the flesh-pots.

17 September

A word in the ear of young writers: reveal your politics at your peril. Remember, nothing goes stale quicker than political controversy, and it is never difficult to fall foul of some party politician posing as a literary critic. But you will ignore my advice, at least I hope you will: because the better the writer the more he or she is a moralist, who cannot stand idly by while politicians govern badly, the innocent are maimed or murdered, the intelligentsia applaud, and the majority as usual supports the wrong side.

18 September

Another spy, an academic doctor at Hull University, is unmasked. He is alleged to have worked for the Stasi, the East German KGB, since 1977. I once wrote a play about spying. William Douglas-Home said there were too many spies in it – no audience could follow or believe in the plot; but recent developments suggest there were too few.

20 September

Last night on TV a programme called *The Spying Game* about Robin Pearson, the Senior Lecturer in Economic and Social History at Hull University, made me feel physically sick. He was – and perhaps is – one of the blinkered brainy fools who voted for marxism. He reminded me of those insects who permit another insect to lay an egg in them, and the egg hatches and becomes a grub and devours the insides of its host. His Stasi controllers destroyed him morally and emotionally: whether he noticed or minded is a moot point. He was paid in roundabout ways for endangering other people's lives; forced into thieving; fell in love with a girl given to him and then taken away by the Stasi; his career was governed by the Stasi, he was a puppet on the Stasi string, and too deeply compromised to escape – retreat was blocked by the threat of blackmail – he was no longer human, a soulless mess. As a Polish lady on the programme put it: 'Spies are filthy.' Pearson has now been unmasked, is disgraced, has lost his job and fled the country. On the programme his controllers – and cronies – were so rational and sympathetic, concealing the dire threats implicit in all they did and have done, that it brought home the terrifying expertise of modern totalitarian methods.

21 September

The longest day of each year is 21 June, the shortest 21 December. In another three months the days will begin to lengthen, lighting up the world and ushering in spring. That is my view anyway; G thinks the end of December ushers in winter.

Jonathan Cecil told me about an Edwardian lady who referred to homosexuals by means of the adjective 'musical'. 'He's musical,' she would say – the nicest possible way of putting it.

22 September

Old dogs, like our Meg, get in the way, young ones are clever at keeping out of it.

A short story entitled *Influence*. Jo, a good-looking woman with modern ideas is twenty-eight and unmarried. She is an only child, has loving parents whom she loves warily, holds down an interesting job with prospects, and lives in a flat she is in the process of buying. But her private adult life has been unsatisfactory. As sensitive girls will, she fell in love with an inadequate young drifter to begin with. After three frustrating years of it she extricated herself and in due course yielded to the overtures of a married man at work. It took her another three years to shake off her selfish lover and celebrate her freedom from the opposite sex. More time passed, and one day she shocked herself by being pleased to be pursued in the street by a rough brute.

Her parents were wise and studious, and had learned the hard way to ask no questions and be told no lies. They met their daughter undemandingly, and she kept her secrets. Jo's childhood home was full of framed family photographs. She noticed a new one of a handsome man of thirty or so. Who was he? A colleague of her father. What was he doing on the mantelpiece? Her mother replied that he had become a friend, had returned from a posting abroad and felt a bit lost, had been their guest as they had been his, was a charming chap, and she had not liked to put his unexpected gift of the photo in a bottom drawer. What was his name? Mark Lincoln.

Ten days later Jo noted that the photo was missing and again interrogated her mother. Where was Mark? Put away. Why? His photo aroused too much curiosity. Were they still seeing him? Oh yes. A day or two later a further question was asked on the telephone. Was she ever going to be allowed to meet the mystery man? The answer was: not a good idea, Mark was supposed to be rather a Romeo, even a Bluebeard.

Then Jo insisted on a meeting with Mark: 'To make sure he's a suitable friend for you two,' meaning for her parents. The consequence was that they fell in love at first sight, or almost first sight, married and lived quite happily ever after. The qualification in respect of their courtship, and the temporary hitch, relate to Jo's discovery of a photograph of herself in Mark's wallet. Where had he got it, she inquired, and he replied: 'Your parents gave it to me and in return I gave them my mugshot.'

At a later stage the pair of couples were watching TV together, a programme about arranged marriages in Pakistan. Jo said: 'I think it's horrible, old people fixing up who the young are and are not to marry.' And the others agreed.

25 September

Manners maketh man, yes – and today's manners sometimes seemeth to make boors of both sexes. Old authors always know a thing or two about manners. They have been snubbed by publishers and abused by journalists. Amongst their occupational hazards are the comments of friends and acquaintances. Here are instances culled from my own experience: a lady said to me, 'I've got your book *Morning* on my library list,' approximately forty years after it was published; versions of 'I'm wading through your book' are commonplace; about my social comedy *Gentleman's Gentleman* somebody said 'It's so sad'; on the other hand my tragic story *A Boy with a Bird* was the cause of laughter. Strangers usually ask, 'Do you write under your own name?' indicating that they have never heard of me. Readers of my 'literary' novels often tell me that their favourite authors write whodunits or ripping yarns or soft porn or pop biogs. I gave one of my books to someone, inscribed and signed it, and five years later my next door neighbour rang to tell me that he had been sent the book by a friend of his, who had bought it in a junk shop in Scotland. Still, I am lucky not yet to have suffered the fate of the late Dormer Creston, whose last book written in her eighties was reviewed by Harold Nicolson and called 'promising'.

26 September

Reading Anthony Beevor's *Stalingrad*. The communists in the USSR were far more repressive than the nazis, and for far longer; but when they fought each other they were equally vile. Incidentally, why has no marxist-communist-socialist country, political leader, propagandist, fellow traveller, soldier, secret policeman, executioner or torturer ever owned up and at least apologised?

27 September

Hosts and hostesses who expect their potential guests to accept their invitations and, having accepted, never to chuck, should be given the widest possible berth. They should not be kowtowed to – you should not feel forced to do their bidding when you feel ill or have more important, if not better, things to do. Decent people, civilised people, acknowledge that there is more to people's lives than is common knowledge and respect the privacy of their friends and acquaintances. A case in point is the sufferer from migraine. He or she is usually unwilling to publicise the illness. They can safely socialise only with persons who are fully informed and/or tolerant. The alternatives are either to be entertained while feeling like death or be quarrelled with. For the migraine sufferers, and their concerned partners, social life is a minefield, and the one impossible route through it is to make no long-range commitments of any kind.

This is the eleventh commandment: thou shalt not die of politeness – meaning, do not let politeness be the death of you, do not imperil your life by observation of the social niceties. Remember, for instance, that many people die at funerals, and that the jest of the elderly after they have witnessed the interment, 'It's hardly worth going home,' is another cautionary tale.

28 September

M has much to grumble about. But she grumbled when she had nothing much to grumble about.

The luckiest people grumble most: is it true? Is it not true?

29 September

I dream of fiction. The story I would like to tell is determined to locate itself in the 1940s, the war years. Every worthwhile writer has looked back in his books, at the years of his youth, about fifty years behind the time at which he is writing. I know my preferred background and atmosphere, and think of a young girl who is simply nice.

30 September

A skit on the literary life in these politically correct days: a would-be author writes about his happy youth, his upper class English God-fearing happily married and loving parents, their home in the country, on a farm inherited from ancestors, and his own perfect marriage to a wife who looks after their children and encourages him in his work. Result – nothing of his gets published. Yet he ends up famous and rich: how come? He begins to benefit by writing that he seemed to remember abuse and beatings by his father, and that he was seduced by his mother. He keeps on changing his religion: he attacks the Church of England, switches to Judaism, turns against the Jews, is converted to Roman Catholicism, satirises the Pope and the Vatican, is momentarily a Muslim, and then becomes a Buddhist preaching at Speakers' Corner on Sundays. His next public move is to accuse his forebears of hard-hearted selfishness, since they accumulated the capital that reared and educated him. He claims that his great-grandfather was black – it had been a family secret, but he had winkled out the truth – and he is therefore a blood- as well as a soul-brother of the race that he most admires. To get away from the snobbery of his family, he seldom washes or shaves and looks like a tramp in photographs. He is strong against all countrified things, the boredom of living in the country and the stupidity of country folk, against farmers, animal husbandry and country sports, and describes the advantages of his new home in a terrace house in the East End, where his best friends are 'real people', criminals and drug addicts. He has left his wife, of course, and tears her limb from limb in books and articles, while boasting about the promiscuity of his sex life. He also makes copy of his battle to gain greater access to his children, who, he complains, have been taught by their mother to fear and hate him. The finishing touches to his great literary reputation are his announcement that he is bisexual, and is leaving this nasty country to spend his last days in the better climate and the more intellectually stimulating society of Miami, USA.

1 October

Down with the cult of the disgusting! What is the point or the charm of metal studs and rings in lips, tongues, nipples and more private parts? They must get in the way of kisses et cetera, will probably cause cancer, and the idea of a painful and dangerous operation having been performed in probably unhygienic premises is the opposite of romantic. Furthermore, people who take dangerous drugs for pleasure and find joy in a hypodermic needle soon look wrong, smell wrong, and do wrong. To be disgusting is not smart, it is disgusting.

2 October

In my little world not all is gloom and doom.

I do not believe I have wasted my life by practising the ancient art of storytelling. I have not lost my faith in the power of the written word, the power for good as well as evil, despite bad books, publishers, journalism and politics. I bow the knee, if rheumatically, before goodness of heart, unselfishness, heroism. I mean to go to church more often, one day, when I am no longer able to offer up my mite of work to the glory of God.

5 October

A nasty great black question mark hangs over the professional prospects of Ben Glazebrook and myself. I have realised that Ben is not going to be able to carry on as before. What is to become of Constable and my friends there? What is to become of Constable's publication of the last two vols of my *Works*? In a bookish context, am I again homeless at my advanced age?

The demon drink crosses my path yet again. My family genes notwithstanding, I have resisted its blandishments to date; but for sixty-odd years I have observed it closely in action, pushing illusions and peddling oblivion. Its votaries are convinced that they can cope with stress better when drunk than sober, can drive better, and are more amusing; that another little drink makes no difference and will do no harm; that they are not addicted to drink and can stop drinking at will; that their unhappy marriages, divorces, sad parents, children and friends, and the fights they get into, are not effects of their alcoholism; and that they are not dying of it.

Syphilis used to be called the English Disease. My guess is that the French called it English in revenge for the male contraceptive being called a 'French letter' in England. Anyway, today the English disease is drunkenness.

7 October

Frosts at night, morning mists rising from the water meadows between us and Newhaven, crisp sunlit days, ever earlier sunsets in red skies.

I am tempted to sponsor an eighth edition of *Morning*. I have sold many copies of my books that ended up in my cellar after their publishers went bust; but they bore the wrong commercial identification, and they are now in short supply. My very own edition could have the right ISBN, making it easier to trace and order. On the other hand, supplying the demands of diligent booksellers and wholesalers would be a development of my cottage industry just when I was thinking of reducing all such commitments.

8 October

Rob, Leslie Robinson, the typographical master-craftsman-artist and the designer of the jackets of my *Works*, also my friend, has sent me a number of mock-ups of possible semi-hard covers of the above-mentioned edition of *Morning*. He thinks it should be a limited and quite luxurious production, whereas my idea was that it should be like a French paperback, and cheap – cheap in price only, I mean and hope.

Spoke to Ben Glazebrook yesterday. He is lunching with me on the 25th.

10 October

Artemis Beevor, née Cooper, daughter of John Julius Norwich who was called Cooper before he inherited his father's title, and grand-daughter of Diana Norwich, formerly Cooper, née Manners, whose maiden name might have been Cust since she was acknowledged to be Harry Cust's daughter – Artemis, as I was saying before I wandered into the wilderness of their aliases, has written a book about Elizabeth David, née Gwynne, a member of the landowning family over Eastbourne way, who became the celebrated cook.

The love of Elizabeth David's life, according to her biographer, was Peter Higgins, my late brother-in-law. Peter's marriage to my half-sister Anne was his second and her third. I believe they were happy together, and she looked after him devotedly when he fell ill. Her story bears out the adage about try, try, try again – the third time can be lucky.

Woodrow Wyatt, who was or pretended to be a fan of my books and whose political journalism I admired, has turned out to be treacherous. Of course he was a turncoat, and, although it was honest of him to broadcast his conversion from socialism to capitalism, turncoats are seldom trustworthy. He divulges all available secrets in his diary, and reveals the infidelity of one of his so-called friends, a male acquaintance of mine. This adulterer was afraid of the reaction of his wife to the revelation that she was sharing him with another woman. Luckily he is also a philosopher, and on second thoughts was glad to remember that his wife was almost illiterate, had never read a book in her life and was unlikely to look into Woodrow's, which has no pictures.

16 October

Paid a visit to the Tring Zoological Museum, housing the collections of a scientific Rothschild. The stuffed creatures are amazing – I was struck by the nine-feet tall bears with four-inch claws, and the huge tigers. The fleas in fancy dress are like Dr Johnson's dancing dog, which did not dance well but was remarkable inasmuch as it danced at all. The fleas can only be studied through a magnifying glass. There are two, one wearing man's clothing, the other a woman's dress. They look like nothing on earth, although their garments seem to be knitted – they are in homely knitwear. They were dressed by a Mexican lady long ago, according to a museum note.

18 October

Yes, yes, I agree, the politicians were to blame for what went wrong with this century. But politicians do not have the brightest ideas: the brightest ideas are dreamed up by art. Having just leafed through a Christie's Magazine showing the 'modern' pictures for sale, I see clearly that Stalin's gulags and Hitler's concentration camps would have been unthinkable, would scarcely have been possible, without art's obliteration of the human body, its beauty, individuality, ideals and yearnings, blood and nerves. Abstract art made men and women into words or numbers or ciphers. The distortions of art taught the world not to take injuries, people in mortal agony, too seriously. Canvases filled with phony writing mocked culture, crazy collages poked fun at logic, spattered paint gave the go-ahead to anarchy, and bare canvases with or without a coat of paint on them carried nihilism to its dead end. What is the point of abstract sculptures? How future generations will laugh at the hideous lumps of metal littering our public places! The worst 'modern' music – or is it the best? – sounds like choruses from the torture chamber.

20 October

My friend W wanted to give his cousin some financial assistance. But the cousin had socialist sympathies, so W, thinking that he was probably against the hereditary principle, asked if he would be embarrassed to accept money by way of inheritance. The cousin said no.

21 October

Tony Blair puts the blame for everything wrong

with this country and this century on 'conservative forces'. Is that a typing error? He must mean 'socialist forces'. Or can he somehow have blanked out the appalling records of the Union of Soviet Socialist Republics and Hitler's National Socialism?

22 October

C J was commissioned by a Russian conductor to write a sort of running commentary on Prokofiev's *Romeo and Juliet* ballet suite, which was to be played in the Royal Albert Hall in a gala in honour of Rudolf Nureyev. Perhaps C J should have smelt a rat – Shakespeare had already done what he was asked to do. The end of the story certainly had a twist. The conductor cancelled the performance in the morning of the day it was to be performed. He had quarrelled with the Russian bass, and flounced out. He – this conductor – was also the sponsor, and is faced with a bill for hire of the hall, for the Royal Philharmonic Orchestra, for participating artists, for C J and the seven thousand or so ticket holders – one million pounds or two or three? What are the odds on his paying up?

24 October

Why buy expensive drugs to make yourself ill? Nature will make you ill for no fee.

26 October

Yesterday I had lunch with Ben Glazebrook. He was like the stag at bay, cornered by the machinations of partners, philosophical in his acceptance of his position, resourcefully planning to extricate himself with a little luck, considering his employees and authors rather than himself, and determined to spare Sara worry. I felt for and admired him. But my future looks bleak: he cannot give the go-ahead for Vols IV and V of my *Collected Works*. I have been suspecting it. I repeated that I would far rather the books came out under the Constable imprint and his control than in any other way. The consolation prize was our agreement that they could be produced by lots of other publishers if the worst came to the worst. Will he succeed in reclaiming something from the wreckage?

27 October

Trollope informed a friend: 'I have written a memoir of my own life and now I feel as though everything were finished and I was ready to go.' In the next six years he wrote fourteen books.

Modern philosophers are not necessarily 'philosophical' in the sense of being wise, kind, privately admirable, and setting the highest standards and the best examples. Bertrand Russell was thought by many to have treated his first wife cruelly and he was certainly unkind to Lady Ottoline Morrell. He was a figure of fun to Rachel Cecil: he came to tea at her childhood home and made passes at her mother under the tea table. Rachel's mother was always scolding him: 'Oh do stop it, Bertie, don't be a bore!' As for Sir Alfred Ayer, meeting him once was more than enough. In my experience he was arrogant, insensitive and rude.

28 October

Iris Murdoch was also a philosopher; but her philosophical cred is marred by the fey strain in her novels and the sudden loss of her grasp of literary reality.

30 October

According to my newspaper Nick Leeson broadcasts the fact that some Dutchmen paid him £60,000 for an hour and a half's talk. Is he lying again, or is the newspaper? He reminds me of the Artful Dodger: he puts all the blame for his crime on the failure of his Barings bosses to catch him. According to that logic, not criminals but the police should be punished for the crimes they have not prevented. His post-penal success story is one of the oldest. The common and not so common people, all the people, have only ever wished to be entertained by monsters.

Times are changing along with the millennium. Homosexuality can now adopt children, it can bathe little boys; has secured its place in the barrack-room; can marry in church, and has many matrimonial rights. Schools will soon be under pressure to teach and preach it. And the age of consent for homosexuals will be lowered to sixteen. The relaxation of tried and tested rules and regulations saddens men who were once pretty boys harried by schoolmasters and lustful youths at boarding schools.

1 November

Morning caused its publisher difficulties because he could not decide whether it was fiction or autobiography. My later books have mostly refused to fit into any precise category or any particular shelf in bookshops – more's the pity, commercially speaking, but thank goodness in other ways. I refuse to be typecast. Lefties call me reactionary, but I was ahead of them in foretelling that communism was a dead letter. Conservative readers shy away from the new-fangled forms of some of my books, *Cautionary Tales for Women*, for example.

2 November

I know the chronology of *The Third Time*, the novel that is still a twinkle in my eye. But will I ever write it? And who will publish it, if not Constable? My friend Vera Brice has both written and spoken to Tweedledum at the Superior Press about my work.

3 November

Is Catherine – Cath – a good name for the heroine of *The Third Time*? Surname: Allen? Another Christian name – Lily? Lily Allen sounds fresh and clean.

4 November

I am too discreet to be a diarist – I cannot bring myself to dish dirt, and deliberately hurt feelings. Alan Clark's caddishness and Woodrow Wyatt's treachery have served their diaries well: monstrosity pays. Parson Woodforde's diary is a list of his dinners, but food must have been his passion and passion is an aid to readability.

5 November

Tonight is Bonfire Night in Lewes. The seventeen Lewes martyrs burned at the stake for their Protestantism will be remembered as well as the failure of the Catholic plot to blow up Parliament. People annually flock into the town from far and wide, the Bonfire Societies march backwards and forwards behind bands from early evening till late at night, there are banners and floats and good-natured anti-popery signs and symbols, then final flurries of fireworks which drive our dogs half-mad. The celebrations deserve support if only because the spoilsports work harder and harder at denying people a bit of fun: the BBC tries to compare Lewes to Northern Ireland, and the cries of bigots, prudes and prigs are that it is politically incorrect, provocative, barbaric, dangerous, orgiastic, noisy, and usually coincides with bad weather. I shall therefore go along to see the sights. Charities get a lot of money from the event.

6 November

Tweedledum of the Superior Press has shown interest in my work and wants to see samples of anything I have written with a London setting; so this morning – without asking questions, for instance why the London connection? – I sent him a letter, a copy of Vol II of my *Works* containing three books including *The Best of Three* which has eight out of its fifteen stories linked to London, and a TS of *Harlequinade*.

8 November

Idea for a short book of manners entitled *How to Grow Old Gracefully*. Here are a few random rules that should be followed by men: keep yourself clean; get your clothes cleaned as often as possible; do not wear rags; invest in new sober-looking garments; no down-at-heel shoes; do not let your hair grow long; buy a magnifying shaving mirror; only grow a beard in special circumstances and when you can have it properly trimmed; beware dandruff; go to the dentist; never say 'It will see me out' or 'I have bought my last overcoat/air ticket/car'; remain aware of your posture; never stoop or shuffle; never hurry; never drink too much or take drugs that change your personality; try not to complain; do not become a monologuist; sympathise with others if possible; be your age!

Ben seems to have opted for going in with Nick Robinson of Robinson Publishers; but I have not spoken to him for some time now.

9 November

A good few of my tips for the older man also apply to women of a certain age, but I would add the following: forget about the passage of time while you remember to exchange your old charms for new ones; yesterday's naughtiness and sulks and pouts will charm no one, and you will have to work harder in order to be popular; steer clear of fashionable clothes; dress to suit your shape; wear trousers with discretion; never even think of shorts; never run anywhere if you can help it; never have a face-lift on the cheap; dye your hair if you must with caution – you will probably regret it anyway; interest yourself in something other than the opposite sex; retain your femininity whatever your sexual orientation; laugh at life however tempting it may be to cry; carry on loving.

Spoke to Ben at last. He has had too many worries to keep everybody informed. He now has hopes of rescue and survival.

10 November

'The hero of my tale ... is truth,' Tolstoy wrote in *Sevastopol*. I have laid claim to a similar aim in my work. The ethics of this century show clearly the 'beauty' – Tolstoy's word – of truth.

11 November

In private life truth without tact can be unbearable.

But in all human relationships, not to mention our relations with animals, lies are hell. Nowadays the matrimonial vows are lies in a large percentage of cases. Egalitarianism is both a popular political cry and a whopper: men always were, are still, and will always be born unequal, and, I hasten to add in the present pedantic climate of opinion, women ditto. Socialism in its charitable, unselfish, anti-capitalist guise is a confidence trick – socialists are as keen to feather their nests as everyone else, and preach that we must do as they say, not as they do. Communism invented organs of repression that were professionally committed to 'brainwash' truth into untruths.

The trouble with truth is that it can be perverted by faith.

13 November

I love our ambiguous language, and ambiguity has figured in various ways in my work. In two books, *Hope Cottage* and *Money Matters*, the narrator of each is disappointed not to have written the book he had in mind, not to have written any book, while his regrets actually add up to one. His notes for the book he had planned are a complete but different book, and the story of his failure is a success inasmuch as it is in print and published – a point often missed.

14 November

I spend more time watching television than

reading. When I was young I read a lot and wrote slowly, later on I began to write a lot and read less. But the admission that I am no longer an avid reader is not another proclamation that the end is nigh for literature. On the contrary, although I watch nonsense on TV which does not affect my work or influence me, I take up a good book with relief. For me the moving image has never been a match for the allure of the written word and its effect on the imagination, and I believe the same must apply to others now and in future.

16 November

The relationships of siblings in their later years are fraught with an accumulation of difficulties. Overlaying the problems of their shared childhoods are the differences of their adult experience, the different interests, the different friends. I knew in my bones that my dear brother and I liked talking to each other on the telephone better than meeting. With my darling sister Rose I had to pretend to be somebody that I no longer was.

17 November

About *Evening*, I fear it has been another casualty – to an extent – of the tribulations of Constable.

18 November

A call from Ben, warning that he was sending me a Press Release by fax. The fax announced the merger of Constable with Robinson Publishing, the creation of Nick Robinson, Jim Lees-Milne's great-nephew. I rang Ben after reading the fax, saying 'I believe I must congratulate you'. He explained that the merger was a rescue operation inasmuch as Nick was moving his whole operation into the Constable premises next month and thus taking over the extremely expensive lease and rental, which otherwise would have ruined Ben and/or bankrupted the company. Murray and Methuen had both rejected a deal because they did not want to move house or help with Ben's rent. He was realistic about the 'clash of cultures' between Constable, an old-style publisher, and Robinson Publishing, a more commercial operation. He said that one of his priorities would be to clear the way for the publication of Vols IV and V of my *Works*, and that he hoped there would be no objections. He would be the Chairman of Constable and Robinson Ltd with a small shareholding and reduced responsibilities. He felt vastly relieved, he said.

This signals a change for me as well as for Constable. What I was waiting for, one of the things I was waiting for, has come to me, as they say in China. It looks as if I may not need to look elsewhere for a publisher willing to complete the edition of my life work (or nearly my life work). A feeling of anti-climax is mainly my response.

Oddly enough, I have never worried much about finding myself without a publisher. I wrote *Memoir in the Middle of the Journey* while pretty sure that Jock Murray would hate its unusual form and reject it, and *Eleanor* after Sinclair-Stevenson Ltd shut up shop and I had no idea where or when it would be published.

I suppose the news from Constable should remove one of the reasons for my marking time in this journal; but I have been bitten too often by publishers not to be shy.

20 November

Cherie Blair aged forty-five is having another baby. Tony Blair or one of his spokesmen has said it was 'unexpected': like the consequences of his political initiatives and acts.

22 November

Covent Garden Opera House has spent some of the money we and others donated to its refurbishment on abolishing the entrance in Floral Street and the staircase that led to the old Royal/Directors' Box and, I think, to one of the balconies. This was done so that all the people must enter in the same way, the egalitarian way, according to some senior spokesperson. How inconvenient! How babyish! But the management continues to charge elitist prices for seats to make up for frittering our money away.

23 November

At least I have served a novelist's apprenticeship

inasmuch as my life has included feast and famine, narrow squeaks, good times and hard times, beds of roses and a palliasse in sundry barrack-rooms for private soldiers, some success and my share of the other – in short, I have inside information about most classes and conditions of existence. When I began to write professionally, one or two people urged me to work my way round the world so as to acquire copy for my stories. My advisers got me wrong. If my writings specialise in anything, I would say it was the female heart.

Nothing from Tweedledum. Why not private publication from now on?

24 November

My *Morning* began as a short story. I plotted almost every sentence of *Tug-of-War*, and spontaneity suffered in consequence. I did not know how *His Christmas Box*, *The Social Comedy*, *Money Matters* and *Evening* ended until I had written everything except the final pages. I announced that *Evening* was my 'last' book largely because I could not again face the strain of composing impromptu, so to speak.

26 November

To cut is half the battle of writing. To have the nerve to cross out, to be hard-hearted enough to part company with your favourite bits, and regret nothing, is half the art as well as the battle. There is no remedy to compare with a cut –

rewriting is unprofessional and inserting afterthoughts is often a mistake.

Good writers do not make good critics of other writers' books. You are one thing or the other. Tolstoy told Chekhov he was a failure. Great critics are rarer than great writers, they have to be more generous.

If you love literature, never read biographies of your dearest authors written in the modern style, that is at enormous length, omitting no personal detail, and without a trace of affection. Great writers are easy to debunk, in the first place they are bound to be strange, and in the second the effort of creating a masterpiece drives most of them mad. Margot Oxford's paradox, 'Genius is closely allied to sanity,' is true in that books of genius display qualities of perception and practical skill that are pre-eminently sane, but misleading in that to preserve the emotional, mental and physical balance required throughout the composition of such work is to strain resources intolerably in most cases. Shakespeare, was he again the greatest exception?

27 November

I became a professional writer not when I began to write for far too many hours a day, nor when I was having a few one-act plays performed on London mini-stages, nor when I set to work on *Morning*, nor even long after that, but when it was much easier for me to write than talk, when

I found out exactly what I had been thinking by writing it down, and was not incurably ashamed of what I had written.

Professionalism is also defined by whenever a writer learns not to take risks. A pro stops before he is exhausted, because he is aware that to take a wrong turning in a piece of work may well be irremediable. A pro knows intuitively how long a book or story or chapter should be, and does not ramble on and cause himself future headaches. A pro has found not only his 'voice', the 'tone' of his writing, the way he can communicate with his readers, he has also found, metaphorically and metaphysically, in his facility for using words and making sentences, a kind of home.

How to exclude ego from a diary? My egoistic answer is that I cannot answer the question. There is another I in the above: please accept my apologies. Yet yours truly would have been glad to get such tips about writing when he was beginning.

28 November

Just over three weeks to the shortest day of the year, hurrah!

The upside of having four Cairn Terriers outweighs the downside; but the downside in the case of Meg begins to outweigh the upside. Meg is fourteen and a half. She now has most of the disabilities that her age suggests, and I personally think her time has come – I mean time for a last trip to the vet. It would be merciful since she now loses her way in our garden and is likely to come to harm one day. Moreover she is blind and we have a lily pool. But occasionally the sweeter side of her nature reasserts itself, and physically she retains her beauty.

Tomorrow to London for lunch with the Glazebrooks.

30 November

Nothing decided. The occasion, our lunch, was very enjoyable, but Ben was unable to say much about the prospects for Vols IV and V – they are largely dependent on Nick Robinson now.

My distant cousin and namesake rang up the night before last. He is one of the four Julian Fanes alive at the present time. He says he is almost blind – he is also deaf. When he asked me what my wife used to be called, he reinterpreted Gilly Swire as Golly Squires.

1 December

It is high time I stopped writing about writing. Listening to those fashionable pseuds gassing about 'doing' their 'art', or rather trying not to listen to them on arts programmes, puts me off.

I shrink from becoming my own publisher so

late in the day. With a little regret, I record what John Crook said to me yesterday evening. He had shown me the Harlequin Edition copies of *The Harrison Archive* produced by himself, text, end papers, binding, everything, and I had signed them on the limitation page, and we were talking over the possibility of our uniting to publish *Harlequinade* and other unwritten books of mine. Referring to the prospect of the marketing and distribution of such books, he said: 'The problem is, we're only interested in trying to create a work of art.'

2 December

Off to Brighton to meet my old friend Val May for lunch and afterwards to a matinée of his production of *The Importance of Being Earnest* at the Theatre Royal. G has never met Val. I have not seen a play directed by him for between forty and fifty years. Yet he and I and a few others shared our youthful aspirations, and he directed my first play, a one-acter entitled *Something Dangerous*: it was about a girl evangelist, genuine or a fraud, torn between sacred and profane love, a melodrama which Val fashioned into a minor success. He went on to direct hundreds of plays here and on Broadway, and is now semi-retired, but exactly as he was in the old days, unspoilt and diffident.

3 December

G and Val took to each other, and we and the

rest of his audience loved his version of Wilde's play, which was labelled foolish and ephemeral by Bernard Shaw a hundred years ago. Val said afterwards that the danger for all involved in staging it is that if the mood or communicative force of a performance is lost there is nothing to hang on to, really no characterisation or even human interest – it is all about blowing bubbles and keeping them in the air. I hope I am not misquoting him. He was complimentary about my work, and amazed by its virtual boycott by the literary establishment that occurred in the middle of my career. He is not much of a reader, except for reading plays, he never was a book reader, but he did read my *Social Comedy*, thought highly of it, and repeated yesterday that it would make a good film, in fact was ready-made for filming. Why was it not in paperback? He pointed out that lip-service is paid by all the arts buffs to the search for quality, quality writing, quality entertainment, yet they ignore my books, the early ones of which were praised to the skies.

6 December

My godson, a successful media consultant, tells me that no best-selling author would think of signing a contract unless £500,000 was guaranteed for 'marketing', to be spent on advertising or hyping the book in question. If true, how literary!

7 December

This morning I rang Tweedledum. Anti-climax

number one, the telephone was not answered for ages; anti-climax two, Tweedledum was in New York. Luckily Vera Brice had given me the name of another Superior Press bigwig, Tweedledee, and I was put through to him. He advised me not to wait for Tweedledum to make up his mind. Still more anti-climactic was his warning that if or when Tweedledum had read my book he would still want others' opinions. No no no – I feel I cannot go back to the proprietor of a publishing house who lacks the confidence or the right to back his own judgment. On the strength or weakness of the above I studied my list of Vera's candidates and picked out Stuart Proffitt, now working at Penguin, and cracked up to be a fine publisher. I rang Penguin. At least someone answered the telephone promptly. But I was then put through to yet another answerphone, on which in no doubt a gloomy tone of voice I left my telephone number. The publishing business has gone downhill since I was involved in it. We were hungrier than today's publishers seem to be, and would not have dared to risk any loss of custom.

9 December

To London tomorrow to lunch with my two British Library ladies, who some years ago accepted the bequest of my archive.

11 December

Lunch yesterday with the Curator of MSS at the

BL, Ann Payne, and the Curator of Modern Literary MSS, Sally Brown. The meetings of our trio have rarity value, since they only happen once a year. We seem to resume exactly where we left off twelve months previously. As always they were full of interesting information about the literary scene in general and morale in museums in particular. Apparently the Government, and specifically the misnamed Department of Culture, have infiltrated representatives of its 'thought police' into museums, who insist on political correctness. Everywhere, the egalitarian levelling is without exception downwards – soon the 'people' will have nothing to admire.

12 December

I have been so busy with practical matters and concern about Vols IV and V that I have hardly spared a thought for *The Third Time*. I would say that my thoughtlessness is the ideal method of plotting and planning a book – it leaves all to the unconscious. Whether or not I am right remains to be seen.

What are Buckies, Chinaman's Hats, Fool's-caps, Piddocks, Quahogs, Tritons, Volutes? Answer: sea shells.

15 December

At Covent Garden Opera for *Falstaff* yesterday evening. The music was as good as ever and the singing fine throughout, but I disliked the production – actually I could not understand chunks of it, and find that I admire Graham Vick and his colleagues less and less.

The refurbished opera house is a vast curate's egg. The best bits from this customer's point of view are the Floral Hall, especially when nearly empty, some of the outlying passages despite low ceilings, and the mercifully unaltered-in-looks auditorium. The bad or worse bits are the heaviness of the main entrance doors, the rather cheerless floorboards that replace the carpet in the stalls, the swirl of chill air-conditioning in Row L on stage left, and unsatisfactory architectural changes to the old Crush Bar. The gents' toilet is a success. I saw no signs of the People's Palace of Blair's vapourings; on the contrary, elitism seemed rather more rampant – our tickets were more expensive, not cheaper.

Our operatic evening was a great treat, setting aside the art and the politics, and we are truly grateful.

16 December

We are going to have a Thai lunch with John and Diana Crook to celebrate the completion of the Harlequin Edition. The first of the fifteen little books was signed by me and published in July 1995, and the fifteenth in December 1999 – the Edition has been roughly three and a half years in the making. John became more expert at printing and binding the books as he went along – they were manufactured from scratch by himself alone in his attic. The layout of text, the quality of marbled end-papers, not to mention the combinations of coloured papers we chose for each title, grew at once more refined and more striking. And the numbers of copies he could produce – between fifteen and thirty – were so small that the whole edition, always a rare item, has now been whittled down to four or five saleable sets.

Still no word from Tweedledum, to whom I wrote on 6 November. Publishers' time differs from our idea of time. Ben Glazebrook's manners are exceptionally good by all standards and perhaps unique in his profession. Jock Murray redeemed many of his failings in my estimation by the courtesy of his letters.

A wild night of wind and rain last night; but we thanked God again for the roof over our heads, and I was comforted by my memories of a book I read as a boy, *At the Back of the North Wind*, which describes sleeping in a hay loft over a stable for carthorses. The wind blew and buffeted in the story, but the young hero is snug and cosy up there in the hay, warmed by the breathing of the great horses below, and lulled to sleep by the movements of their hooves on the straw and cobbles, and their companionable equine equivalent of snores.

18 December

How to write about love nowadays? Nearly all the sexual frontiers have been crossed by writers through the ages and in our century. I cannot help feeling that even pent-up voyeurs have had enough of hackneyed sex scenes in books, and actors and actresses heaving and groaning in cinemas and in our homes on TV. All love stories are different, however small the difference, but sex boils down to being roughly the same. Bad writers and cheap film makers may make money by ignoring that fact of life – artists can no longer do so, they have to find other ways of redefining romanticism.

The latest cinematic fashion is that the woman undresses the man – she does it with the expertise of a prostitute although she may be acting the part of a teenage virgin, whereas in real life most people know that male clothing is nearly as mysterious as female, buttons often refuse to go through buttonholes, ties get knotted, zips catch in shirt-tails, in pants and even in penises, and trousers cannot be pulled over shoes. The more natural proceeding, that the man undresses the woman, is apparently old hat. Lovers in films seldom get into bed: the climate in Hollywood is warmer than the climate in Carlisle or Inverness; and towels, such an important adjunct to adultery, are conspicuously absent. Film lovers sleep entangled together, post-coitally: not an insomniac, not a restless writher, let alone a thunderous snorer, amongst them.

19 December

Sensuality has a hard time of it in the busy world of today. Most men, what with work in the money mill, TV, sport and possibly paternity, have time only for the quickest of sexual fixes. The art of seduction, in modern lingo 'foreplay', is confined to the Australian model: 'Brace yourself, Sheila!' But quick fixes quickly become boring in a book, except maybe for schoolchildren of all ages. Courtship, not consummation, is the real stuff of love stories, and, in a sense, of fiction in general. The best books now have to have recourse to the secret language, the intimate signals, that arouse – and possibly please – sophisticated readers. Film directors will have to try to be more subtle and present the dramas enacted by eyes; the sexual capabilities of lips and smiles; the power to excite of the movements of hands; and remember that the removal of a necktie or a woman's rings or earrings or spectacles, can be more of a thrill than seeing paid performers doing sexual gym in the altogether.

Neurosis has a field day with sex. The unpredictability of neurotics drives their lovers round one bend or another. Neurotics are too keen on sex or too averse to it, or often both. They are apt to enslave their partners by means of the aphrodisiac of their sudden changes of heart, and the effect on their other bodily organs. Their love-making is the more intense because they fear it may be the last time, because it is additionally fired by desperation, guilt and contrition – they are trying to make up for all the trouble they have caused. They are dangerous people, they as it were carry a fatal infection, and their partners, although they may say adieu and retreat and flee, can easily find that those individualistic kisses and nights of wistful passion are irreplaceable.

Love need not be consummated to be consuming. Chateaubriand is supposed never to have possessed Madame Recamier, although they were lovers for years and she spent so much time on a *chaise longue*. She is supposed to have said that if she had given all of herself to him she would have lost him, meaning that as he was or had been a potent womaniser she kept on pleasing him by offering something different. The love-life of French sophisticates is not a firm foundation for generalisations about sex or no sex. Yet in cold climates the same phenomenon is recorded. Hazlitt in his intriguing *Liber Amoris* describes his enslavement by a chit of a girl he scarcely touched. And I know of representatives of both sexes who hang on to normal healthy lovers in spite of ruling out fun and games.

20 December

The 'emancipation' of women gets two cheers. The third cheer is held back because 'emancipation' suggests love has been unshackled, that love is at last free, and free love is one of the benefits won by the revolt of the fair sex. H G Wells preached and practised it, and men have been giving tongue ever since. But, even while women run countries and are at liberty to sleep around, bear illegitimate babies, and join men's clubs, the emotional and physiological conditions of their lives, and in innumerable cases their material and financial welfare, are exactly the same as they always have been; and to think otherwise is asking for trouble.

21 December

The Church of England is under a three-pronged attack, first and foremost from the enemy within, who have censored the poetry in the Bible, and introduced absurd and embarrassing practices into its services; secondly from its homosexual priests, the consequent publicity, and the muddle about it all at the top; and thirdly from the spoilt population of this affluent country, and the facile and shallow cynicism of its media people who pull long noses at any person or institution unlikely to answer back.

To call the spirit of the age iconoclastic would be to dignify what is more like street wit and anarchy. Respect for virtue is a dead or dying letter – and what is sacred? Blasphemy is a new line in music-hall patter. Our Queen is mocked for serving her people with lifelong and selfless devotion, and republicans bare their teeth at her while – in my lifetime – presidential despots, tyrants, homicidal maniacs, sadists, embezzlers, thieves and lunatics, not to mention the warmongers, the alcoholics, the satyrs, rule other countries and usually escape punishment for their crimes.

A young man of my acquaintance, well-favoured and clever, was repeatedly either pushed out or walked out of good jobs, deserted lovely and loving girlfriends or was given his marching orders, switched sides politically, changed his mind, came to grief and seemed incapable of mending or seeing the need to mend his ways. A friend of his and mine explained that he 'had a little problem with authority' – a brilliant and charitable description of square pegs, rebels without a cause, members of the awkward squad, and class warriors – the worst people and sometimes the best.

23 December

Rejection slip – actually a peculiar and even illiterate letter – written on behalf of Tweedledum probably by an office boy being cared for in the community of the Superior Press.

24 December

It is Christmas Eve, and a second letter arrived from the Superior Press today, translating the first into English. Tweedledum has taken about six weeks to tell me that he has no room in his list for my work. Yet, via Vera Brice, he invited me to submit that work.

* * *

Cooking tomorrow instead of writing – we shall be in the kitchen, preparing to feed my sister June, husband Jeremy and son Christopher. Happy Christmas everyone!

26 December

We went to church yesterday morning. The officiating priest read the Communion Service well, but his explanation of the Nativity managed to translate a mystery into an enigma. Anyway, I gave thanks for my many blessings, not least for the one – G – who knelt beside me.

27 December

It would be against the odds that Eng. Lit. will do much in a world-beating way in the foreseeable future. Our glory days ended half a century ago, our language is showing signs of decrepitude, and we are no longer a united kingdom. Great books are written as a rule in nations where conditions prevail that are the exact opposite of ours.

Doubtless – probably – possibly – maybe! After all, the millennium is just round the corner, the fate of prophets is often to be proved wrong, and temperamentally I need to strike a positive note. There is no telling, nor foretelling, what good writers will write. There are flowers of autumn as well as of spring. There is even good work that has emerged from the ends of centuries, when civilisations are apt to break up and break down.

30 December

Subject for a novel: a girl of good family rebels against parents, siblings, home, school, and feels lost and angry. She gravitates to a psychiatrist, who hears her out over a year or two of sessions, then tells her to make peace with the world. This is not what she wanted to hear, so she goes to another psychiatrist, and another and another. At last she finds one who satisfies her: his message is that she is right and everybody else is wrong, she must vent her anger on all the people she is angry with, express her hatreds, get all the bile out of her system. How does the story end? It would be poetic justice if the girl turned on her evil genius and exposed him in a book or newspaper.

31 December

The writer Malcolm Bradbury is urging fellow-writers to forsake their computers and take up the pencil instead, so perhaps I have been at the cutting edge of literary technology all along without knowing it.

We will be celebrating the birth of Jesus and the beginning of Christianity tonight. The two Christian millennia are a blink of the eye of time. But religion has existed as long as we have, and all religions unite in defending us from death.

I wish I was a better Christian – I owe Christianity

a bigger debt than I have repaid, though I have tried to stand up for it in my books. It helped me through many crises in my life, and I hope it will do so in the days ahead.

1 January 2000

We saw the old year out and the new millennium in at Glyndebourne. It is not possible to thank the Christie family adequately for all the enjoyment they have given us and a good few million others. There was a party on the stage for the permanent company and friends of the Christies. In the enormous stage area tables for ten were arranged under spectacular lighting, spotlit pools of light for each table. The tables were beautifully laid around central vases filled with white paper chrysanthemums, trailing ivy and theatrical golden spikes – the chrysanthemums were those used on the stage sets of *Pelléas and Mélisande* and *The Bartered Bride.* There were a couple of large TV screens which would show the ceremonies in London at midnight. The schedule was tight: we had to sit down to dinner and finish eating on various dots. All was good, all went smoothly, and the generosity over wines and liquid refreshments was lavish. Then we had speeches and a cabaret performed by the stars of international opera. When they stopped, our attention switched to the TV screens, and eventually the clock for a second or two showed '00'. Cheers from everywhere – G was with me and we embraced. Kisses and good wishes were exchanged generally – Auld Lang Syne was being sung on the telly – and the high decibel band for dancing struck up. It was time for us to leave, and we said as many goodbyes as possible and drove home through the deserted and peaceful streets of Lewes to find we had not been burgled.

EXTRA TIME

2001

1 January 2001

Where was I?

Oh yes – a whole year has passed – and after a night disturbed by fireworks – last one heard between 2 and 3 a.m. – I am trying to remember all the loose ends left dangling by my 1999 diary.

2 January

Our hometown Lewes has a Chinese-style passion for fireworks. Any excuse is a good excuse for my neighbours to let off a few. Not only the dogs of Lewes have had enough of sights and sounds that mimic war.

To recap: Ben Glazebrook's company Constable merged with Robinson Books – Constable and Robinson Ltd was created. But Nick Robinson ruled out the publication of fiction – no more proper novels – which meant that the last two volumes of my *Collected Works* were disallowed and would not get into print.

However, Ben urged me to be patient. And in the first six months of last year, 2000, he was pleased to report increasingly close co-operation between Constable and Robinson. At last, after an interruption of about fifteen months, Ben obtained Nick Robinson's agreement to honour my contracts and complete the edition. The two books in question are now in the final stages of production and are due out in June of this year, thanks be and much to my relief.

12 January

Ten days have passed since my last entry. We went to Venice to celebrate our silver wedding, where I was attacked by vertigo. Venice was the up, we had spent our honeymoon there, my giddiness and nausea were the down. But how lucky we are to have been in Venice, and how lucky I am to be able to stand up straight, courtesy of some little white pills and the NHS!

Venice was flooded repeatedly during our four-day visit. Dinner on the last night of our stay was served by waiters in waders – they had to wade through a flooded area to reach the kitchen.

To carry on from where I left off ten days ago: last year I managed to publish personally the 8th edition of *Morning*. It was originally launched by John Murray in 1956. Nearly fifty years later it still sells in small quantities. To keep it alive, and looking better than in any of its previous incarnations, had been an ambition of mine for months. Leslie Robinson and Vera Brice, the latter presiding over the Production Department of Harper Collins, designed the 8th edition. The imprint used, St George's Press, derives from the company of the same name which I helped to found and, in time, voluntarily to wind up – St George's Press is also the name of my cottage industry of selling back numbers of my books. At last the finished article, two hundred and fifty numbered copies signed by the author, in a superior jacketed paperback format much admired by connoisseurs, burst upon the wide world last September.

The tally so far is that I retain just under two hundred copies, which suits me quite well, taking the long-term view. The exercise has been successful in my own estimation – not too many downs in the context. But I had never before published anything of my own, and now I am in a position to join in the chorus of advisers against doing it yourself. Here again I was lucky – my text was not vandalised by uncorrected errors like Proust's, nor was I conned or robbed as colleagues of mine have been. The fact remains that the slog involved, and the risks and responsibilities incurred, are incommensurate with the rewards in my own case and, I suspect, in the great majority of cases.

The next slices of my literary life are typical of all my recent experience. In 1999, while writing *Marking Time*, I itched to stop keeping a diary and to go back to fiction. Eventually I did so, brought forth the novella I had been gestating, *The Third Time*, and immediately wished to, and then did, write two more novellas, *The First Nail* and *The Last Straw*. Each was forty-odd thousand words in length, as against sixty to eighty thousand for a full-length modern novel, and I hoped to get them published separately, making three short books – after all, nobody nowadays is supposed to be able to concentrate on anything for more than minutes.

13 January

Ben Glazebrook read *The Third Time* and approved of it, but, as was established following the merger of Constable with Robinson, he was no longer in a position to publish fiction. After many sheltered years with St George's Press and Hamish Hamilton Ltd and Constable, I was on my own in the literary jungle, armed with nothing more than advice from friends that some of the wild beasts might be kinder than others. I contacted six publishers: with one exception they behaved atrociously. My letters were not answered, my telephone calls were ignored, the publishers misled me or lied, had no manners, were as contrary as spoilt children, venal yet missing the point of remunerative offers, knew nothing and, again by my standards, had closed minds and no imagination. If there should ever be a genuine study of the decadence of English literature in the second half of the twentieth century, students would find most of the information required by looking at the majority not of writers but of publishers. The lone exception to the above, while I was searching for someone to publish me, rejected *The Third Time* with grace and regrets, and for reasons beyond his control.

At that point I gave up – I had neither the time nor the inclination to be treated like dirt. Despite the strain and stress I would do the job myself. Again, my friendly experts gathered round and supplied suggestions and estimates. The best suggestion was to do the three books in paperback with black titles on red covers, and sell them either separately or in a semi-transparent plastic box. But the cost of a production of that sort was prohibitive. And however the books were produced, the problem of distribution remained – they would have to be marketed, not buried in my cellar. Two distributors were recommended to me: one never responded to my inquiry, which might have put money in his pocket, the other was so extraordinarily pessimistic and defeatist that I was pleased to say to him, 'No, thanks'.

In the middle of all this, late last autumn, the proofs of Volumes IV and V of my *Collected Works* arrived. Proof-reading approximately half a million words was both a distraction and satisfactory.

But when the 10 kg of printed matter had been posted back to Constable I was confronted by the same problem. What was to become of my possibly final, and unusually fecund, year's work? The long up of the joys of creation began to deteriorate into the down of fearing that the destination of my three stories might be my bottom drawer or wastepaper basket.

I mentioned my difficulty to yet another friend, who asked why I had not spoken to the Book Guild.

Suffice it to add for the present that I am now waiting to clinch a contract for the publication in a single volume of my three *Tales of Love and War* by the Book Guild of Lewes.

14 January

Last night on the four main earth-bound channels of television, as I zapped from one to the other as quickly as I could, I was disgusted by relentless references to excrement. Not only the adult morons of today's entertainment industry are attracted verbally to faeces and sewage, the lumpen-intelligentsia follow the fashion. A theatrical producer at the top of his particular tree, while producing a high comedy written by a famous foreign playwright and translated by a friend of mine, inserted rude words in the text and introduced farting into the action.

15 January

Here is a list of Queen Victoria's descendants who have surprising nicknames: 'Affie', Duke of Edinburgh and Coburg, d 1900; 'Liko', Prince Henry of Battenberg, d 1896; 'Ernie', Grand Duke of Hesse, d 1937; 'Alicky', Tsarina of Russia, murdered 1918; 'Mossy', Princess of Hesse, d 1941; 'Nando', King of Rumania, d 1927; 'Ducky', Grand Duchess of Hesse, d 1936.

18 January

I cannot say I am sorry that Auberon Waugh is dead. The hoary adage about not speaking ill of the departed is absurd – can one not say that Adolf Hitler was a devil? Waugh carried on a vendetta against me and my work for many years. I have no idea why, I never met or had words with him or wrote to him. Some would suggest that he thought my writing so bad that he wished to censor it out of existence; but I have published at least four times as many books as he did, have had a five volume collected edition of my books published while still alive, and his sister Harriet Waugh wrote a charming review of my *Happy Endings*. I think he must have been as crazy as his father, though much less gifted. Long ago Patsy Grigg reported to me that she had met Waugh at some dinner party and remonstrated with him for denigrating me in different ways, to which he replied: 'A lot of people say the same thing, and the more they say it the more I shall denigrate' – or words to that effect. More recently he got himself invited to stay at Badminton, where he sat next to my sister-in-law at dinner. The next morning my sister-in-law rang to ask me: 'What on earth have you done to Auberon Waugh?' – a question referring to his public diatribe against me. In the distant past he reviewed one or two of my books in an extremely patronising way, but I did not object to being called 'a silly boy' in spite of my seniority. Again, he showed his scorn or his spite by commissioning a duke with no literary credentials to write a review of my book about my mother for his magazine. Evelyn Waugh and son did not like competitors: Evelyn at once snubbed his contemporary writers and indulged his psychopathic snobbery by claiming that the drunken ramblings of aristocratic Henry Green's autobiography was the best of books. Auberon Waugh's obituarists have written that he was a generous friend. Be that as it may, he was a mean self-appointed enemy.

Met Carol Biss at the Book Guild yesterday morning. The publication of my *Tales of Love and War* is now in the bag, barring a signature on the contract. Hurrah! And hurrah not least for having found an impressive managing director of a publishing house located some five hundred yards from my study.

20 January

I owe my last literary harbour and haven to Miles Jebb, our friend, the author and editor, and now, following the death of his father, Lord Gladwyn.

Six weeks ago I was on the verge of throwing in the towel in the sense of consigning my three novellas to perdition. Then Miles told me that George and Jane Nissen had acquired The Book Guild. The reputation of Jane Nissen swung it for me: without delay I rang her up, and now I am about to become a Book Guild author. Jane Nissen was in charge of the Children's Books at Hamish Hamilton while I was part-published by the same firm. Everybody spoke well of her and admired her record as publisher. I once submitted a children's story for her consideration, and received a letter rejecting it that caused more pleasure than pain. As soon as Miles mentioned the Nissens' name, I was confident that an enterprise in which Jane was involved could not be bad.

Contracts are due to be signed in three days. Thank you, Miles! Here's hoping the story has a happy ending.

Reading a most interesting book, *Explaining Hitler* by Ron Rosenbaum. It is wonderfully researched, well written, and has taught me much that I did not know, despite my interest in the subject. Rosenbaum quotes from *The Portage to San Cristobal of A.H.* by George Steiner. I imagine that Steiner was aware that his two letters of the alphabet, which refer to Adolf Hitler, were used to describe the anus in the English vernacular of my youth, and were regularly applied to raw recruits in the army by sergeant-majors.

21 January

I presume to think I can understand why the Jews have created an industry of research into why they were 'chosen' to be sacrificed in the Holocaust. But could it be that they are pushing their 'explanations' of Hitler to Byzantine extremes? He was wicked, he was evil, and evil does not need to be argued over, the facts describe it, common sense recognises it, and perhaps in an ultimate definition it is what is inexplicable.

Liberal opinion denies the existence of evil. Liberal opinions are the Achilles heel of Jewry in the twentieth century. Karl Marx, born a Jew, reheated the Christian potage and served it up with liberal trimmings, class war leading to heaven on earth – no need to die in order to get into the marxist heaven. Jews fell for it: they played a large part in the October Revolution and in leninism and even stalinism, and were mostly liquidated for their pains. They have run with the hare of capitalism and hunted with the hounds of socialism in western democracies ever since.

The paragraph above reminds me of my late brother-in-law, the concert pianist Franz Osborn. He was a card-carrying communist in Germany, where his family had lived for generations, but fled in the nick of time, reached England as a refugee, and belatedly became the most right-wing of conservatives. Arthur Koestler ditto – he was a communist activist in his native Germany, also in Spain, and became an arch-conservative in England. They were two of the many who worshipped the God that failed.

Liberals believe people called evil are misunderstood. They cannot stomach the idea of original sin. They cling to their faith in the notion that human beings will always behave themselves, given the chance. The consequences have been that liberal optimism, gullibility, naivety opened the door for the tyrants. Is liberalism on guard against an always possible revolt against fallible democratic governance and the rise of evil politicians promising to get rid of criminals and make the trains run on time? Is it – hell!

* * *

The banner headline of *Dog World* (7.4.2000), WHIPPET MURDERS, referred to the murdered mother and daughter who bred whippets.

22 January

Eileen Short died. She was our daily lady for several years long ago. We became friends and kept our friendship going. She was a spinster, plain, overweight, clever, cheerful and ribald. She was not known by many, and will soon be forgotten except by a few. But she was a heroine. She was a heroine of unselfishness. She had a dotty brother, who was put in an institution when his and Eileen's parents died. He was unhappy there, so Eileen said she would look after him in the family home. She did so for twenty-seven years, during which he went madder than usual at full moons and was apt to use violence against her. He clung to her, he was always able to beg her not to return him to the institution, and she never complained and never abandoned him.

24 January

This afternoon I am due to sign a contract with the Book Guild for my thirty-seventh book. The BG has treated me from the word go with exceptional respect and courtesy.

A pet parrot was ill. Its owner took it to a vet who specialised in parrots' ailments. The waiting-room was full of other parrots and their owners. All the parrots were doing their tricks: one sang 'I did it my way', another 'Greensleeves', a third kept on saying 'Pretty boy', a fourth 'Bugger off', a fifth imitated the ring of a telephone, a sixth wolf-whistled.

27 January

We do not travel much. G seems to have been everywhere and I am a stick-in-the-mud, like my mother. She laughed at travellers bringing home more or less nasty infections, and hard-line stories of hours of waiting for planes and trains, of traffic jams, missed connections, stolen luggage and unexpected weather. Very late in life she agreed to go and stay with friends in Holland. She was accompanied by a much younger and stronger female acquaintance. On the second night of the visit the young and strong acquaintance suddenly died. My mother was confirmed in her view that it was better to stay put.

A sunny day – what is the world coming to? We have been rained on for weeks. The water meadows between us and Newhaven are flooded. I hope my long-suffering neighbours and friends who live in Cliffe and Malling – parts of Lewes – have not had more mucky water in their homes. The birds are unaware of the plight of our town. They have been singing since before Christmas. I love song-birds, and hate to see so many magpies and even jays spying out the nests soon to provide them with hot dinners.

30 January

Neither a borrower nor a raconteur be.

1 February

G found the diary she had kept when she was about ten years old. It was such a slim volume that only one ruled line was provided for each daily entry. Her writing was therefore limited to the briefest record of the outstanding event of each day. These examples of two-day sequences certainly convey an impression of time flying: here is one, 'Stayed in bed ... Went shopping', or again, 'A (her brother Adrian Swire) went to school ... A's school burned down'.

I have been acquainted with two women who share the distinction of living with husbands but paying with their own money for their own food. The absurdities and the miseries of the war of the sexes will never be fully chronicled or known.

2 February

'Mistress' has become a taboo word. A woman living in sin with a man is a 'lover' now – no discrimination between her and her opposite number. And homosexual partners are both 'lovers'. 'Lover' comes in handy in a different context. The vernacular uses it in negative sentences: 'I'm not a lover of Banoffee Pie ... I can't say I'm a lover of poisonous snakes.'

3 February

My preparations for going abroad on holiday in six days are pathetic. My pleasantry to the effect that I might as well be going to the next world is hardly an exaggeration.

4 February

I cannot claim that sociability is my second nature. Most practitioners of arts have difficulty with social rites and obligations. Although my family tree is decorated with amateur writers, I never met a professional artist until I was nineteen years old. He was Edward Seago, the painter, whose secretary I became for six months half a century ago. In those days Ted Seago guarded his privacy fiercely and fairly successfully. But later I think he was appalled by the high price of fame, and was driven demented by having to put in personal appearances, and by intrusive admirers and fans. He quarrelled with people who had bought his pictures – he was always prepared to hurt feelings in order to be free to get on with his work.

Ted Seago died in his early sixties. He was born with a heart condition, but died of cancer. It was another of the ironies that must have been written in his stars.

He was the younger of his parents' two children. His elder brother John was the favourite, and Ted was the weakling, who cost the family a fortune in doctors' bills. But John ended up as an impecunious bore, while Ted gritted his teeth and supported his philistine father and malicious mother for many years.

Ted sold his first picture aged sixteen, and not long afterwards, as soon as he could scratch a living, resisted all parental pressure and left home. He acquired technical wizardry, and became extraordinarily prolific. That he was patronised or ignored by the aesthetes, critics and crooks who ran the modern art market during his lifetime, distressed and then embittered him. But he had won his immortality.

5 February

Ted Seago, owing to his productivity, painted some pictures that were better than others, or, vice versa, some that were less good. He had a tendency to hark back to sentimental rustic scenes of a bygone age, and often accused himself of having a picture postcard mentality. Actually, as a rule, his pictorial imagination was romantic and refined, especially so in his native Norfolk studies. But I was young when I worked for him, did not take the range of his work into consideration and was grudging in my praise of his hay carts in the sunset and ploughing with horses in a flock of seagulls. Now I regret my error, having learnt that artists worthy of the name need and merit encouragement.

Ted's father was a coal-merchant and smallholder. I would classify him as a yeoman. Ted's mother was or thought herself a cut above: when Mr

Seago wrote her letters during his courtship, she returned them with the grammar and spelling corrected in red ink. A remarkable artist was an unlikely consequence of their pairing. Are all artists changelings?

Another painter taught me a lesson about the artist's life. A friend of mine wrote to Augustus John begging him for a picture to be sold in aid of some charity and to attend the auction in person. He wrote back to refuse. He stated that he had no pictures to spare and never turned up at society dos. He added that his sister Gwen had ruined herself by giving away her pictures, and wrecked her work and her health by responding to every appeal for help.

26 February

Just back from our fortnight's holiday in France. We flew to and from Nice: the flight lasts about two hours whereas any other form of transport would take much longer. Flying is convenient from the temporal point of view, but is thoroughly inconvenient otherwise. Big airports always seem to be miles away from one's point of departure, delays are apparently inevitable and too long however short, muddle is customary, discomfort is par for the course, and then there is the fear of getting and being airborne. Modern travel is supposed to be better in all respects than it used to be, but whether or not it is safer and more dependable than it was in the eighteenth century is a moot point.

* * *

On our holiday I read two books by Kingsley Amis. One, *The Green Man*, is a conventional ghost story but quite clever, the other, *The Riverside Villas Murder*, is ridiculously far-fetched. The prose of both is workaday, but in *The Green Man* it is packed with cynicism, in the *Murder* it falls apart at the seams. *The Green Man* was first published in 1969, the other book four years later. What a decline! Was it due to drink? The personality of the writer that emerges from both books is disagreeable and despairing.

I was shocked to see that C P Snow, my friend Charles Snow, whose weakness it was to think he was or soon would be the king of the literary castle, heaps fulsome praise on that potboiler *The Riverside Villas Murder*.

28 February

My unhappy country – now a foot and mouth epidemic and ruination faced by many of those who feed us!

1 March

This March has come in like the most mangy and miserable of lions – uniformly grey sky and snowy drizzle, another rail crash, news bad – so for pity's sake let it go out like a lamb happier than those being killed and burned along with other livestock on the countrywide funeral pyres (science's high-tech remedy for the foot and mouth disease).

* * *

While on holiday I jotted down ideas for entries in my diary. I did likewise when I was writing fiction. But such ideas have never been any use to me. On the contrary, they turn out to be red herrings. In my own opinion my best work has been a spontaneous record of a train of thought shunted along on a daily basis. The suggestions of my holiday persona feel like interference by a stranger.

Here are a few of the delightful names of the pioneers of jazz: Cannonball Adderley, Big Bill Broonzy, Wayman Carver, Ornette Coleman, Dusko Goykovitch, Huddie Ledbetter, Fate Marable, Miff Mole, Dudu Pukwana, Pinetop Smith.

2 March

Two newcomers into the rude vernacular: first, the Americanism 'Wow!', an exclamation signifying surprise, also pain or pleasure, sorrow or joy, fear or any feeling thought to be indescribable by means of the spoken word; and secondly 'There you go', meaning 'Here you are ... Eat your dinner ... I've done what you asked me to do' etc. The latter is friendly, but, like 'Wow!', so imprecise as to resemble a neigh or a grunt.

On the other hand, a faint sign of hope worthy of a 'Wow!' and a 'There you go': the daughter of a carpenter friend of ours walked out of her job at a bank because of the filthy language of the bank manager. More employees should follow her example. The people who work in the media should all refuse to peddle swear-words and smut. Actresses should not imitate copulation – they should not be blackmailed to do so. Journalists should clamber out of the gutter, and self-styled artists should not be encouraged to disgrace art. Pigs should learn to fly.

4 March

A true statistic for a change: no less than ten members of our circle of acquaintances are more or less involved with criminals in and out of prison. Is it idealism? Is it slumming? Does do-gooding do any good? Undoubtedly women have a dangerously soft spot for criminals.

5 March

A shorn head used to be a mark of shame meted out to wrongdoers. Nowadays, some people choose to cut off their hair for more or less good reasons. But skulls are seldom nice to look at, and as a fashion accessory are a flop, also in bad taste because of the link with illness.

6 March

Alan Ross died while we were on holiday. He was gifted and gallant. He ran the London Magazine for years on a mysterious shoestring, and published one of my stories. The LM was the last respectable literary magazine, and may continue to be so. Alan lent it some of his own quirky character. His quirkiness was exemplified by the 'art' photographs he chose to publish in many issues: as a rule they were extremely banal – of shoppers queuing for a bus, or a schoolboy in the middle distance – and the reproduction was 'grainy' almost to the point of invisibility.

The unpalatable truth for egalitarians is that you have to get about in smart society, and mix with the wealthy, in order to obtain the backing for idealistic ventures in support of art. Capitalism is the 'only begetter' of the best art. God bless the patrons! Alan was a class act, as they say nowadays, in both the editorial and the fund-raising contexts.

Egalitarianism promotes insubordination.

7 March

I would like to write in praise of my wife. Many a diary has done GBH to wives: for instances, John Osborne's with its repeated references to the wife he called Adolf, and Alan Clark's with his boasts of having betrayed Jane, and Jim Lees-Milne's which blames Alvilde for standing in the way of his homosexual affairs. The trouble is that writing is a means of getting something out of your system, and that is exactly the opposite of what I was thinking of in relation to G. The most I dare to put on paper is that her unselfishness knows no bounds: which might as well be written in invisible ink since not many people will appreciate the dimensions of the compliment.

* * *

John Crook is coming to teach us how to use our computer this afternoon. The three questions that arise are – will it be any good for me, will G let it replace her beloved typewriter, and will we ever master it? I could never do creative work on a computer – the appearance of my hand-written pages, the age-old act of making my mark on a receptive medium, are an essential part of the process. I speak for myself – but again with thanks to Malcolm Bradbury for having publicly argued that computers are the enemy of art.

9 March

I woke in the night, was convinced it was morning and struggled not to fall asleep again. It must have been two o'clock. I realised my mistake round about three, failed to readjust and get back to sleep, and seemed to become a compendium of every ailment in the medical dictionary (of which we do not possess a copy).

One night I dreamt of the unsavoury title of a book which I hope has not been written and never will be: *Feet in Hot Weather, The Odorific Conditions known to Podology.*

10 March

Talking of fools, BBC 2 rushed in yesterday evening with a programme about class. A narrator claimed that the end of World War II at long last gave merit its chance and ushered in the rule of a brand new meritocracy. What rot! Most of the hereditary peers in the House of Lords were and are descended from meritocrats. The Establishment was, is and will be meritocratic. The class system in England defeats analysis, and certainly defeated BBC 2. Its mystery is its charm and its strength. The upper class – aristocracy by another name – is indestructible and timeless. High society during the French Revolution differed from the high society it was destroying by nothing but its cast of characters. Napoleon could not wait to reign as emperor, supported by those whom he ennobled. Lenin and Stalin were tsars, and both were more imperious and terrible than Ivan. And meritocrats nearly always do their level best to pass on their privileges to their offspring in a universal and natural manner.

A clever friend of my youth identified the disability of the English proletariat to speak English, and its cause, as early as 1945. They speak without closing their mouths, and either adenoids or laziness or both complete the formation of 'peasantalk'. Thus they say 'fi' and chi' for fish and chips. 'Ho' equals hullo, and of course 'Hi' suits them to a t. Here are up to date translations of a few common phrases: 'Wa dri'?' = Want a drink? 'Wi you ma me?' = Will you marry me? 'E ma bi' = He's my baby. 'I yad nutt i' = I had enough of it. 'Bi'nd good ri t'ba rish' = Goodbye and good riddance to bad rubbish.

11 March

Pigeon-holing is not exclusively reserved for pigeons. People never have stopped, and never will, cramming their fellows into races and classes, into psychological straitjackets, and divisions reserved for sheep and goats. To discriminate is just about the first function of being. Later, it often poses a political threat. But in between it can be socially entertaining. Isaiah Berlin had a pigeon-hole for those who experience mental events and those who experience none. David and Rachel Cecil invented a category of 'leprechauns', who live in worlds of their own.

12 March

My bookshelves are full of signed copies of good books that are dodos. What became of P Anthony Spalding? He produced *A Reader's Handbook to Proust*, an essential reference book for as long as *A La Recherche* is read; but his fascinating *In the Margin, Extracts from a Bookman's Notebook*, published probably privately round about 1960, caused a stir amongst the cognoscenti and has sunk without a trace. The novels of C P Snow are out of print, I believe. L P Hartley's masterpiece *The Boat* is unobtainable. Does anyone read the poetry of the painter David Jones, once admired although nobody could make head or tail of it? Are T S Eliot's prose musings read nowadays, and is the courageous vivacity of Joyce Cary's fiction another victim of time? Better to write for fun, to amuse ourselves, than for will-o'-the-wisps like posterity, fame, success or money!

13 March

We live in a country decaying, disunited, nearly bankrupt, and governed by leaders who like to pose disastrously as Good Samaritans. Where would be a better place to live?

14 March

My *Tales of Love and War* has arrived, copy-edited and marked up, and I must try to concentrate on it.

24 March

For ten days I have been finally revising the typescript of my *Tales*. I worked according to my wont, that is hard, and as a result was exhausted. The occupational hazard of old age is to think it is capable.

Another mistake in the losing battle with time was exemplified by a deaf old boy who came to tea with us. He apologised for his deafness, but said he never wore his four-thousand-pound deaf aid, he could not abide the thing, he could not get used to it, and thought it did not improve his hearing. Result – he was a menace. He could hear nothing, demanded repeat performances of our every pleasantry, strained our vocal cords, and obviously should have stayed at home. My sister Anne and lots of friends learn to manage their aids – often supplied by the NHS – discreetly, and are not noticeable doornails.

I have never liked revising my books. It is such a strain to bottle up the creative impulse and hand over to the critical faculty.

25 March

A sad story: Aggie married Bert, a postman. They were plain people in every sense, and had no children – she was disgusted by sex and his sex drive was minimal. They rubbed along in a dim and dull way until they were each getting on for fifty. Then their friend and neighbour Tom, a widower who owned the other half of their semi-detached property, resigned from his job in local government, went to live with his daughter in another town, and rented out his house. Tom's tenant was a dashing young man, handsome and black-haired, Desmond by name. Aggie fancied Desmond – it had never happened to her before. She spoke to him if she could, spied on him, treasured his smiles, wove daydreams round his fine figure. He drove an open-top red sports car, and one Saturday afternoon in summer he brought a blonde woman home. Aggie happened to be in her bedroom at the time, therefore looked down on the couple through her net curtains. They were talking and laughing at something, Desmond and that woman, and she leant across and stuffed her hand through the waistband of his trousers. A few moments later she withdrew her hand, they both got out of the car and hurried into the house.

This scene, witnessed by Aggie, led to her writing to Tom to complain of his tenant. Desmond was keeping bad company, she told Tom, and bringing their shared premises into disrepute. She did not leave it at that. Ignoring the attempts of poor old Tom and his daughter to placate her, she bombarded them with complaints about Desmond's garbage, loud music, late hours, and especially his female visitors who were clearly prostitutes and the disgusting noises that penetrated party walls.

She vented her spleen on Desmond himself, but in sneaky ways. She poured weed killer on his front lawn at night, and blamed vandals. She scratched his car with a nail. She blackguarded him in local shops. At weekends she rang him from phone boxes in hopes of interrupting sexual intercourse. And she persuaded Bert to pinch his mail from the sorting office, so that she could steam open the envelopes and read the letters – Bert did it to stop her nagging him to death.

Eventually Desmond moved out, whether or not because of Aggie's activities.

She was stricken. She shed bitter tears by the bucketful. She could not sleep or eat, and banished Bert from their bedroom. At last he took her almost by force to see their doctor. The doctor gave her a few pills to counteract the symptoms of the change of life and promised that she would soon be right as rain.

Reading a biography of F. Scott Fitzgerald by a certain André le Vot. In accordance with the biographical fashion, it is too long and detailed; but the story survives its treatment. FSF must be the most extreme modern example of the classic syndrome of genius and idiocy unified in one person. Zelda, his wife, exemplifies another type, and was possibly the model of the neurotic Southern Belles who figure in the plays of Tennessee Williams. Her dicing with death is breathtaking. His stupidity and alcoholism likewise.

26 March

FSF was an alcoholic, Zelda drank too much. Drink, and no doubt harder drugs, make and break talented people. Van Gogh explained to his brother that he could not have used the colour yellow as he had done if he had not been drunk. Malcolm Lowry owed his *Under the Volcano* to his alcoholic experience; the same applies to Patrick Hamilton's *Hangover Square* and Charles Jackson's *The Lost Weekend* – but there are too many examples to list. Insensibility, self-induced and chronic, is apparently as inspirational as sensibility. Whatever is closely related to death – religion, love, politics, war, and natural and unnatural illness – always inspires. Zelda went mad and died in a fire at a sanatorium.

Back in touch with Emmanuel College at Cambridge. I wrote to my friend and former Master of the College, Derek Brewer, professor and poet, some weeks ago to say that the edition of my *Collected Works* would be completed in the summer and I was thinking of donating a set of the five volumes to Emmanuel. He advised me to speak to the new full-time Emmanuel librarian, Dr Helen Carron.

I did so last week, and gave her the briefest possible history lesson, as follows. My forebears founded and endowed Emmanuel College, from which Harvard University sprang. Consequently, about a decade ago, I offered to bequeath my Archive to it, plus bequest. The then Master, Derek Brewer, accepted the offer and metaphorically welcomed me with open arms. But Derek retired, and a new master, Norman St John Stevas, ennobled in the guise of Lord St John, took over. I soon noticed a lack of interest in me and mine; and Norman was markedly uncommunicative. At length I wrote to him to say I felt neglected and wondered whether Emmanuel still wanted my Archive. Answer came there none: I waited for a few months and then approached the British Library, offering the same deal. It was accepted with alacrity and enthusiasm. When Norman eventually wrote to the effect that the College longed to receive my bequest, I could reply that he had missed the boat, the BL would be the recipient.

Dr Carron assured me that Emmanuel would be pleased to have a copy of my *Collected Works*. I then mentioned my condition, since I was twice shy of giving to the ungrateful. Could I have an introduction to the Harvard Library? Intriguing to see what happens next.

29 March

The astronomers, scientists and damn nearly everybody else are dying to know if there is intelligent life on another planet. The much more pressing question is whether there is intelligent life on ours.

30 March

Old people always fall over. I took my second tumble last night. I was carrying our faithful old dog Dulcie down brick steps on to our garden lawn. It had been raining as usual, my feet slipped from under me, and I crashed down, but apparently my left hand took most of the strain. That hand and particularly the left wrist are more or less painful, though no bones seem to be broken. Otherwise, a grazed right elbow, nothing else so far – I have been lucky. But there are the unpredictable effects of shock to look forward to.

Incidentally, the shock for Dulcie must have been as bad or even worse than it was for me. She was flung from the arms of the master who had always previously been kind and gentle. After my fall, while still prostrate on the steps, I was pleased to see her squatting to relieve herself in a flowerbed some six inches from my face.

31 March

Left hand and wrist swollen, but no longer so painful. Possibly due to shock I slept yesterday morning, again in the afternoon, and some nine hours last night.

Nearing the end of the Scott Fitzgerald biography at last. His latter days were terrible. He had been loved and envied, rich and famous, then he could not afford to eat, was a hopeless wino, a fighting drunk, and his fine books were out of print. He had great dignity yet could behave in the most undignified and intolerable ways.

One of the many interesting things in the story of his life is the nastiness of Ernest Hemingway. I know the Hemingway type, and that it is to be avoided, if possible. Ernest competed meanly with Scott, and showed malice towards him. Ernest was all for masculinity, masculine activities and sports, and the courage of brave men, but he was a bitch at heart. He despised and condemned Scott for doing his best to destroy himself, yet in due course he committed suicide.

Beautiful writing is difficult to define, but unmistakable by those who have the eye and ear to be moved by it. The eye is dazzled by sentences that carry neatness, precision, individuality and charm to astral levels. The ear can hear the melodious and haunting rhythm of their cadences. The psyche is seduced as if by a siren's song which beckons us not against rocks but into a new and better world.

The letter of the alphabet most closely linked

with love is v, v for Venus and venereal, vulva and vagina.

1 April

Not feeling up to much today, is it shock or hypochondria?

3 April

My reaction to falling flat on my back on brick steps was to go to sleep – I have had hours and hours of sleep in the last few days and nights. Think I am quite normal today, but wonder if others would agree.

4 April

Not so normal yesterday as I liked to think I was. Vitality ran out, stamina proved to be in short supply. Blood pressure must have sunk through the floor.

6 April

Received a letter from Dr Carron, Librarian at Emmanuel College. She thanked for the copy of *A Reader's Choice* I had sent her – it is Diana Crook's anthology of excerpts from my books. Dr C wrote to say she had included it in an exhibition of books etc that bear upon the founding of Emmanuel – I was in with my forefathers. She also informed me that she had forwarded the other copy of *A Reader's Choice* that I had sent her to the Widener Library, part of the Harvard Library: which is just about all I had hoped for.

The Last Illusion, a story I have in mind, which will probably remain there, would or could go like this: a young woman called Jane with literary leanings aspires to become a professional writer. She sets about making her wish come true by seeking the advice of established authors and critics and commentators. The letters she writes them are flattering, she declares that she has regarded their writings as positively godlike, that she longs to become their disciple or, in terms of authorship, their protégée, and she encloses a revealing photograph of her nubile charms. For the next six or seven years she services over-sexed scribes and media men in their studies and offices. At the end of that busy period she produces a slim volume: it is reviewed glowingly and widely – which of her important lovers would dare to displease a girl who has dirty stories to tell and sell? Jane's book sales, then her appearances on TV, at first in literary programmes, next in chat shows, game shows, advertisements for lipstick, make her famous or at any rate notorious. But she is no slacker, her pen and her person are harder at it than ever. In the next twenty-odd years she runs through generations of useful lovers and publishes a few blockbusters based upon her wide experience of the opposite sex. Alas, the change of life pumps her up to three times the size she had been when she was pretty and powerful. And she can write nothing – once upon a time her men put in stints of post-coital creative editorial work on her books. She is afraid to go out, and stays at home to cry in front of the mirror. She is lonely, she has never needed to marry, and now she would not lower herself so far as to wed the types that pity and propose to her. But years pass, her courage revives, and she takes up her pen again. She writes letters to her old friends to ask for advice about the autobiography she is contemplating. Immediately she is not only remembered but in demand, propositioned this time round to serve on quangos, committees, prize juries, supply forewords and compile anthologies, and eventually to receive prizes and honours for her lifelong dedication to the cause of literature. She never writes her autobiography – it is superfluous to requirements, she enjoys the honourable niche she has carved for herself in the world of letters and art. She takes to public speaking, gives talks to PEN and at out of the way universities. The burden of her message to writers in general and the young ones in particular is that they must make their mark by talent and nothing else.

An heroic journalist called Minette Marin writes in *The Daily Telegraph* today that 'allowing women into something is usually a sign of institutional decline. That has been the way with the Church of England, men's clubs, MI5 and the armed services'. Where is the hero or heroine who will include in Minette's list many of the jobs associated with literature?

9 April

A story called *Dreams* could be shorter than short. A woman divorces her husband, who is a charming rogue, and marries a second husband whom she cannot fault. She claims to be perfectly happy; but in her dreams she still loves her first husband and is sorry that she got rid of him.

Reading Montherlant's *The Bachelors* (*Les Celibataires*), a great book by a great writer. What a joy to read something so good, what a relief to be reminded that great writing exists! The translation by my friendly acquaintance Peter Quennell seems to be worthy of the original.

12 April

Easter approaches.

I was extremely religious between the ages of twelve and fourteen when – and because – I was unhappy at school. Often since then, but intermittently, God has been my friend in need – my need, not His. Nowadays my prayers include apologies.

In various books I have written about the sort of religion I subscribe to. The funerals of atheists must be responsible for many conversions to belief in a god of some kind. Science answers none of the riddles of the universe so far. My bet is that God will stay well ahead of the scientists.

13 April, Good Friday

Strange that Good Friday should fall on a Friday the thirteenth.

This is the weekend that retells one of the seven great stories, the story of *resurrection*, death and resurrection of Jesus, and of redemption. On lower levels it is also the story of rags to riches, of Cinderella, and the story I have told in most or even all of my writings. But, although I am not ashamed of having tried to cheer people up, I am well aware that the story of resurrection, not the tenet of Christian faith but the story in a general sense, can be inverted – millions, billions, the casualties of the twentieth century, would deny the possibility of endings happy in a personal mundane form. Older age specialises in appreciation of the negative sides of the six other great stories: absence of *love*, not so much *conflict* as surrender, not so much *recognition* as blindness, a reluctance to discover anything by means of *exploration*, no *faith*, and not enough *generosity*.

I write my diary in Extra Time, two words borrowed from the rules of football, referring to the period of play after two teams have finished their game without one scoring more than the other. The particular relevance of the phrase to my circumstances is that I am writing here and now after the game of my life's work was or seemed to be done. When I wrote *Evening*, someone asked: 'What about *Night?*' When I told someone about *Extra Time*, I was asked: 'Is *Injury Time* next?'

15 April

Before I gave a talk the other day the gentleman who introduced me told the following story. He said his name was Walter Allen, and he recently attended the graduation ceremony at a university where his son had studied. His son warned him that car parking would be a problem, but on the day he arrived early and noticed an empty space in a car park close to the place of assembly. He drove towards it and was stopped by an attendant, who asked his name. He supplied it, and was waved into the aforesaid space politely. He then met his son, took his seat, and watched the long-drawn-out business of the awards of degrees. Eventually the man in charge of the proceedings made an announcement. He apologised on behalf of the guest of honour, the eminent academic Professor Walter Allen, who was hoping soon to arrive and deliver his address as planned – he had been looking for somewhere to park his car for the last hour and a half.

17 April

Religion equals choice. You can choose to be religious or irreligious. You can choose to be married in church, you can have a downbeat atheist's funeral. Your life, your private life, is dependent on choosing, on the exercise of free will. It is all your own fault, apart from the workings of nature, the whims of politicians, and accidents.

20 April

Finished copies of the two last volumes of the *Collected Works* arrived this morning, and make everything worthwhile. By everything, I mean all that has happened between Ben's tentative proposal over lunch six or seven years ago and the sight of the five vols in my study. The problems of finance were solved. The design of the dustjackets by Leslie Robinson and Vera Brice is perfect. Ben survived the assaults on his company and rescued it with assistance from Robinson Publishing. Both Ben and I withstood attacks on our health. Of course there are things that could be better, there always are, especially in the writing of the fifteen separate books included in the five vols; but it is too late to worry, and whatever happens to my work once it is available to readers is really not my business. A huge thank you to the talented people who contributed to the venture, and supported me as I stumbled towards the finishing line of what often seemed a marathon too far.

24 April

One of my see-saw days yesterday. In the morning I worked well, and in the afternoon we went to a nursery garden and found and bought the few plants we were looking for. The sun shone, it was a balmy spring day with blossom and birdsong. After tea we went to Seaford for a walk beside the calm sea, and later I rang my sister Anne in Spain. She sounded mortally ill. She ended by thanking me for having always been kind to her – a sad signal. She has wished in vain to die ever since she lost her husband Peter Higgins.

25 April

Rang Anne this a.m. She sounded bright and belligerent. I had almost buried her.

27 April

What are Aristotle's Lantern, Cobbler, Corkwing, Father-lasher, Medusa, Pogge, Shanny and White Cat?
    Answer, creatures of the watery world.
    Aristotle's Lantern is part of the sea urchin. Cobbler is a fish of the sea-scorpion family, and a Father-lasher and a Pogge are others. A Corkwing is a fish called wrasse. A Medusa is a jellyfish. A Shanny is a blenny, and a blenny is like a stickleback. A White Cat is a nasty-looking worm.

Arts are easily lost. Draughtsmanship went to the dogs in the last century: is there a revival? The writing of fine English prose is history: I generalise, but compare the sentences of two best-selling authors, Sir Walter Scott and Ian Fleming, in order to see what I mean. William Douglas-Home explained to me that all the prose in his plays had a distinctive rhythm, but that usually the directors of his plays and most of the actors failed to grasp it. No contemporary literary critic to my knowledge has ever commented perceptively on a writer's prose, and I would guess that no more than one in a thousand members of the public could tell the difference between journalese and an elegant sentence. The New English Bible is the sin against the Holy Ghost in this context.

28 April

Tolstoy thought that a person's appearance, whether it was considered good-looking or bad-looking by people in general and by himself or herself in particular, and especially if it did or did not find favour with the opposite sex, formed that person's character, outlook, opinions, fortunes, happiness, and might actually make history in one way or another.

Alas, the savage spinsters, growing old ungracefully, with nothing to boast about except their quarrels, so sharp that they continue to cut themselves, biting every hand that would feed them, and amazed that they have been condemned to die alone and largely of their loneliness!

Some spinsters lead the happiest of lives, thanks to their characters.

29 April

Tomorrow to London to lunch with my nephew, the jeweller Harry Fane, my brother's second son. He and his elder brother are getting more interested in our family history. I have nothing against Fanes, but feel myself more in tune with my mother's family. A strange episode occurred some fifty years ago. I was at home, at Lyegrove in Gloucestershire, had been chopping wood on a winter's afternoon, and was walking back to the house through the gathering dusk. On entering the house I found my mother and her sister, my aunt Laura Lovat, in distress. Apparently they had been drawing the curtains, saw me in the drive, and were afraid that I was the ghost of their father, the Lord Ribblesdale painted by Sargent. They thought I looked like him. Certainly I share his ascetic tastes and love of literature.

Before jotting down the above I referred to the Extinct Peerages section of the 1956 Burke's *Peerage, Baronetage and Knightage.* The entry under Ribblesdale, my grandfather, omitted the eldest of his three daughters. She was Barbara Wilson, Wilson being her married name, who wrote several excellent books, including the highly praised *Dear Youth.* Such is life and death for writers.

1 May

Riots expected today in London. The rioters are rioting against those who pay the taxes that provide the money that pays the dole that enables them to riot on a working weekday.

A story describing one couple's attempts to plumb the mysteries of the marriage of another couple, and the mistakes they inevitably make.

2 May

The novelist who writes a diary cannot pretend to be someone else – there are no closets to hide in, the motley must be set aside, birthday suits are the order of the day. He or she is under pressure to use the first person singular in an unaccustomed manner. Consequently I feel honour bound to confess that both my parents were, in today's jargon, toffs. I belong in the class pigeonhole reserved for fairly modern English writers together with the Sitwells, Siegfried Sassoon, George Orwell, Byron, Shelley and Walter Scott. Similar foreign types are Dante, Goethe, Pushkin, Tolstoy and nearly all the great writers of Russia's Marvellous Decade. I believe my work has sometimes been sneered at for non-literary reasons, just as, in the good old days, Byron sneered at Keats for being plebeian.

3 May

Apparently the riot in London cost about twenty million pounds worth of damage. The Civil Liberties brigade is arguing that the police should have allowed the hooligans to do more.

6 May

Domestic sins, crimes and misdemeanours, what are they? I mean not GBH or illegal activities, but those traits of personality and those habits which are difficult to live with. Husbands who lunch at home are supposed to be providing cause for divorce. A bully can be intolerable, likewise a drunkard, a gambler, a spendthrift, a bore, or a sharp-tongued or plaintive spouse. An oppressive father, a proprietorial mother, uncaring parents, parents who divorce, all play havoc with young lives.

On a more personal level some people are allergic to dirty minds, fingernails, tricks. My wise old friend Violet Schiff thought that flippancy was a great mistake. Teasing that hurts is definitely a no no. And watch the face of the partner of a raconteur, who is listening to the same story for the umpteenth time!

In my opinion unresponsiveness is deadly. It is the antonym of charm. It is charmless; you cannot communicate with it; nothing excuses it – absent-mindedness, other preoccupations; it is the worst of bad manners; it is a killer. The powerful and impatient, the insensitive and inconsiderate, the clever-clever and the stupid-stupid may think that they get away with not bothering to respond: they are wrong, they are loathed and not forgiven.

The cruelty of innumerable episodes of the cull of livestock, unhealthy and healthy, to cure the national herd of foot and mouth, has elicited not a squeak of protest from the RSPCA, the animal rights terrorists, the anti-vivisectionists, the anti-fox hunting mob, the ignorant animal lovers who finance these organisations, the millionaires who pay for illegal violence against law-abiding scientists and sportsmen, and above all the media.

7 May

Hard cheese for atheists! In the 1962 edition of Roget's *Thesaurus* thirty-eight column inches approx. (960 mm) are devoted to the names of Gods, of the Divinities of various religions in various countries in the various ages. Unbelief and doubt, on the other hand, get four inches (100 mm), and irreligion another four inches.

8 May

The election for 7 June to be announced today. God help us all!

On a summer's day two Chelsea Pensioners rested on a seat in the King's Road, watching the girls in miniskirts and flimsy dresses go by. One Pensioner said to the other in a wheezy old voice, 'You remember that stuff they put in our tea when we were in the army – bromide, they called it – to stop us feeling fruity? Well, I'm afraid it's starting to work.'

9 May

When I was a boy my favourite birds were falcons and hawks. Then I graduated to liking owls best. Now my favourites are swallows and especially swifts.

Swifts are mysterious and romantic. They fly beautifully, know their way across the world, and their cries are summery and sound joyful.

Not well today.

12 May

My indisposition which was mildly gastric has turned into shingles.

Unknown words that describe a fool: calf, tony, Tom Noddy, moonraker, sawney, beetle-head, numps.

13 May

Human inconsistency has a field day during a political election. Some self-made millionaires, the odd lottery winner, and persons dependent on capitalism from birth, also those who would starve if the rich got poorer, and social snobs fighting tooth and nail for status, are proud to proclaim that they will vote for socialism, which aims to redistribute wealth and do away with class distinctions.

16 May

When the body hurts, mind has a job to overrule matter. But heroes managed it, Keats, Proust, Denton Welch. And creative work is better for you than nothing.

17 May

Sam Goldwyn, the Hollywood mogul, is said to have said: 'Nobody ever lost money by underestimating the taste and intelligence of the public.' This is clearly the advice followed by the popular media in my alien country.

This evening the Glyndebourne Festival opens with *Fidelio*.

18 May

Again *Fidelio* moved me, because of Beethoven, Simon Rattle and good singers. The producer, Deborah Warner, is quite contrary. She is contrary to abolish the season of the year, spring, referred to in the libretto; not noticeably to release the prisoners into the fresh air, the open air, which they gratefully sing about; and to dress the prisoners, their gaoler and the prison governor in identical modern attire, which makes the story difficult to follow – actually, I believe the governor's clothes are even more slovenly than those of his 'servant', the gaoler. In Act II she places the action not in a prison 'vault' but in a huge unconfined space – no walls or ceiling; and finally she drops snowflakes on the entire company of thinly clad 'Spaniards'.

I do not forget that I am lucky to have had the chance to discuss the work of Miss Warner.

21 May

Shingles not an aid to keeping a diary.

Reading a thriller by the best-selling American author James Hall, whose writing has been highly praised internationally. My estimate is that versions of the word 'fuck' occur at least one thousand times in its three hundred-odd pages.

22 May

'Ask no favours, lose no friends': if that is not already a proverb, it ought to become one.

Britten's *Midsummer Night's Dream*, Peter Hall's production thereof, revived in memory of its designer John Bury, equals another enchanted Glyndebourne evening.

25 May

My seventy-fourth birthday.

Luckily for me I am like my mother, who took no notice of anniversaries or the passage of time. I rather think she died of a ninetieth birthday party my brother gave for her – it suddenly reminded her of how old she was and that it would be impolite to keep death waiting.

* * *

I have turned against paperback books belatedly. They began well, but have become the repository of all the trash masquerading as literature. There are many more bad books than good books in paperback. Their boast is that they are cheap – they should be ashamed of how cheap most of them are. And they fall apart and the paper they are written on turns yellow and decays.

26 May

For that matter, following on from the intolerant entry above, I marvel that the majority of writers should be willing to cede control over their work to the kind of middlemen and middlewomen I have come across. The literary agents known to me and my friends were apt to take no trouble if there seemed to be no money in a book. Moreover they were judge and jury in respect of work submitted to them, although usually without discernible literary qualifications. Unconstrained by responsibility, they must have sealed the fate of innumerable writers.

Again, a very few exceptions have proved the rule to me that publishers are a low form of life. I allow that they must take financial risks, and no doubt have wives and children to feed, but do they need to be disobliging, both sheeplike and reckless, and to play fast and loose with authors' hearts, souls and interests? Publishing was meant to be the profession of gentlemen once upon a time.

There is an alternative to putting all your artistic eggs into the baskets proffered by agents and publishers. You can retain a smaller or larger share of the process of publication of your work. That means expenditure of money in cash or loss of money in contractual form. Money is difficult but not impossible to raise – I speak from experience. I became a publisher myself in order to get my books published as I wished, and my investment in the business was virtually nil, neither I nor my two colleagues, Carlo Ardito and Michael Hatwell, invested a penny in it (see my book *How to Publish Yourself*).

27 May

Night thoughts on yesterday's entry: I must issue a warning about writers employed by publishing houses – they are most unlikely to appreciate or be well-disposed to other writers' work – the story of Andre Gide's rejection of Proust's *Swann's Way* for the worst reasons is typical.

28 May

Down with the Kennel Club! It sets the standards for the various breeds of dogs, and appoints the judges for Crufts, and the consequences are the crippled hindquarters of German Shepherd Dogs; dogs blinded by their drooping upper eyelids; other dogs with drooping and inflamed lower eyelids; Bulldogs with such big heads that they cannot reproduce naturally; Poodles with foxy muzzles; Pugs and Pekingese with such short noses that they are incapable of breathing properly, and so on ad nauseam. But the Kennel Club will have to mend its ways – foreign dogs that are better looking than English ones are now able to compete here.

2 June

A story called *The Man Who Cared for Women*. The father dies young, and the son takes care of his mother. He feels for her in her widowhood, shoulders her burdens, protects and cheers her as best he can and devotes himself to her welfare. But when he is seventeen she remarries, and her second husband is an architect who gets a job in Saudi Arabia and drags her off to live there. The boy is bereft and bewildered – how can his mother opt to take the sort of risks from which he has shielded her? Some years pass, and he finds Miss Right. She is charming and suffering from her parents' divorce. He promises her security, that he will look after her always, and she promises never to desert him. They marry and are happy. But then she becomes pregnant. He worries about her day and night, and dreads the dangers of parturition. The birth is far worse than he anticipated – he is driven half mad by her protracted agony and rages against her doctors, the baby and even herself. And she does not survive and his daughter dies. He has been doubly deserted, deserted yet again, and decides that women are not to be trusted – all his care of them is in vain. Many more years pass, and he marries once more, doubts notwithstanding. She is much younger than he is – he can guide her through life; and she is poorer – he can provide for her. She is a career girl in a small way and is grateful for his support. But as a result of her marriage and her new-found confidence she wins promotion and works twice as hard in a more responsible job. She comes home exhausted on weekday evenings and spends weekends in bed with migraines. He urges her to rest, see a doctor, look for less stressful employment, and begins to be cross with her for not heeding his advice. His nagging, as she calls it, is a bone of contention between them. In the course of a terminal row he accuses her of being masochistic and of not letting him save her from herself; whereupon she retorts that he has never really cared for her or, she suspects, for anyone else, all he cares about is to stop people upsetting his own peace of mind.

Election notes: two socialist households in our street advertise their political sympathies with posters. The houses they have recently bought cost in the region of £500,000.

6 June

Adults to seven-year-old boy: 'Do you like your school? ... Are you happy at school? ... Have you got lots of school friends? ... Is the work hard at your school?'

Seven-year-old boy under his breath: 'School, school, school – I know enough!'

Character is worth more than cleverness in the longer term.

10 June

If you want to know how painful it can be to put on a soft cotton shirt, get shingles.

20 June

Brave artists, Tom Stoppard, for example, are beginning to speak out against the meaningless messes of what claims to be 'conceptual art'.

The stuff that is on show in some of the great London galleries is bad enough, but go into the country, into the new towns, and see the abortions presuming and presumed to be art that have been commissioned by councillors and clerks of the works!

22 June

The proof of the dust jacket for *Tales of Love and War* is pretty, but bears no relation whatsoever to the text of the book. It must contravene the Trade Descriptions Act.

23 June

I have never written about the famous people I have known, setting aside the four subjects of my *Best Friends*. This diary is not exactly autobiographical, nor a scandal sheet, nor a gallery of thumbnail sketches – and may therefore be less amusing than it could have been. But now, rightly or wrongly, I feel obliged to throw my own flicker of light on history before it is too late.

26 June

The Book Guild is proving to be the most obliging of all my publishers. Because that dust jacket of my *Tales of Love and War* has no connection with the stories in the book but is otherwise eye-catching, Janet Wrench immediately suggests getting another design from a different artist.

27 June

As I was saying or writing, this seems to be the place for my memories of the mighty. Winston Churchill was a small man, surprisingly so, not least because his ducal cousins of younger generations were and are bean-poles. He must have suffered from his small stature, height being considered the prerequisite of gentility in some snobbish quarters. He looked to me like a clever version of a mixture of Mr Pickwick and Jorrocks. I met him only once – he was old, in the pink of health, forceful and with some magnetism. I saw no sign of his social boorishness – my mother once walked out of a luncheon party because she had been seated next to him and he refused to speak to her.

Anthony Eden was a friend of friends of mine, as a result I was included in two Sunday lunches at his last home in the country. They were memorable in different ways. The first convinced me that he was the most charming man I had met – and I have not changed my mind since then. He was outstandingly handsome, and intelligent and responsive – he had the sensibility of an artist, no doubt inherited partly from his father who painted well. And he was more than polite to me because of a strange link between us: my grandfather Lord Ribblesdale and his father Sir William Eden, the bad-tempered subject of *The Tribulations of a Baronet* written by his son and heir Timothy, both rented suites of rooms in Rosa Lewis' notorious Cavendish Hotel in Jermyn Street – between them they gave Rosa her start as an eccentric hotelier. However, my second lunch verged on the disastrous. Another guest, a politician, was late and Anthony Eden over-reacted – his chronic ill health asserted itself, he was impatient and cross. His wife Clarissa behaved admirably and calmed him down as best she could; but at lunch he was provoked into trying to justify the Suez fiasco that ended his political career. It was a disillusionment for me. He died soon afterwards. He was created Earl of Avon and had every kind of decoration, including an MC for valour.

Harold Macmillan was genial and wanted to know what I thought about things when I was too young to have thoughts about anything – I might have been nineteen when I met him. He was reputed to be a very good shot and an expert billiards player. Although he was considered by some to be too easy-going and lax as Prime Minister, after retiring on the grounds of ill-health he took up the reins again at his family publishing business and reorganised it ruthlessly.

Hugh Gaitskell, an academic and socialist who led the Labour Party, betrayed his political principles and probably his wife by succumbing to the wiles of an aristocratic society hostess, married thirdly at the relevant period to Ian Fleming, the creator of James Bond. Anne Fleming gave parties in her elegant house in Victoria Square, to one of which I was invited. Gaitskell was not included; but, in accordance with the rumours, he joined us after fighting under the red flag in the House of Commons, shared Anne's chair at the head of her luxurious dining-table and drank coffee out of her coffee cup.

When I met Prime Minister Margaret Thatcher, she startled as well as pleased me by saying she had a soft spot for Fanes. She explained that she had been at school with a girl who asked her out to tea at her home near Grantham: the girl was my distant cousin, a member of the Fane family of Fulbeck, Lincolnshire, and her home was Fulbeck Hall. Mrs Thatcher, as she then was, Lady Thatcher as she is, said she thought Fulbeck Hall marvellous and that she had never forgotten the kindness of its owners. Margaret Thatcher rose far above the prejudices of male chauvinists and snobs, of jealous feminists and women, and was an exceptionally good English politician with common sense and an admirable character. Her husband Denis had perfect manners and tact.

28 June

Those historical literary cliques amaze me. I cannot believe that Thomas Mann in Hollywood benefited from reading aloud his work in progress to Einstein, Chaplin and other luminaries. Editorial assistance usually tolls the knell for real writing. Creative writers talk too much at their peril. A literary vocation requires you to be alone, search your heart in solitude, and never lay your life-work before outsiders or the public until it is complete, unchangeable, and proof against critics and meddlers.

Drink looms large in my memories of artists – other drugs too, probably, but mainly drink. Harold Nicolson and Vita Sackville-West were never sober when I met them, Leslie Hartley died of drink, Evelyn Waugh likewise by all accounts, John Betjeman over-indulged, Philip Toynbee was an alcoholic – the list could be endless.

Harold and Vita and John Betjeman were true friends of my work. Harold had a red face and a moustache and could have been in command of a regiment, judging by his looks; but his heart was soft, not martial, his temperament was all tenderness and generosity, and he was the most modest of men, considering his achievements. When I thanked him for his help in getting my first book *Morning* published, he said something to the effect that his greatest pleasure was to promote the work of young writers more talented than he himself was.

The Nicolsons exemplified the potentially successful union of male and female homosexuals. Vita was a manly figure with big hands and feet, Harold's hands were small and his feet looked tiny in his suede shoes. She was enchanting when sober and a bully when drunk, and Harold was willing to be bullied – he let her wreck both his diplomatic and political careers. They were an odd couple, she the haughty aristocrat and poet, he the journeyman born and bred. They stuck together largely by living apart – he was in London during the week, and at Sissinghurst at weekends they occupied different houses. They also stuck together by post, by their correspondence, and apparently by their tolerance of each other's sexual proclivities.

My friend Cynthia Asquith told me a story that illustrates Vita's masculine ideology. Simon, Cynthia's son, said to Ben Nicolson, Vita's son, 'My mother complains that I drink too much and have too many women,' to which Ben replied, 'My mother complains that I don't drink enough and don't have enough women.'

29 June

John Betjeman is indescribable – he was a mild case of the multi-personality syndrome. He was a road-hog, the most competitive of drivers; yet extraordinarily generous to young hopefuls in his own field. He was convivial, yet reserved and hid behind his jokes and laughter. He was loveable, but tested the patience of those who loved him with his demands for service and attention. He was part teddy bear part tyrant. I was very fond of him – he was not only kind to me, he understood everything.

In connection with the Nicolsons I think of the Pope-Hennessy brothers, yet can find no record of either of them in any of my reference books. They were the arch-intellectuals of the cultural scene in my youth, John the authority on painting and architecture, the big cheese in the world of museums, and James the social favourite who combined scholarship with dining out, the biographer par excellence, and now their work is superseded, they are dead, buried, forgotten, and I apologise to their shades if I have misspelt their name.

John was the most superior, apparently arrogant, unapproachable and awkward of social presences. He looked down his nose and deigned scarcely to speak to anyone outside his precious circle. I tried to read a book of his the other day, *Aspects of Provence*, which I hoped would be more accessible than he had ever been and than I imagined his tomes on art were. It was hopeless, academic beyond bearing, history run riot, a leaden touch throughout and no encouragement to anyone to go anywhere in that delightful region of France.

James was a close friend of Harold and Vita, and perhaps John was too. They all had art and their sexual orientations in common. But James deteriorated rapidly and painfully until he was murdered. He looked Malayan – there had surely been a slip-up in his forebears' consular activities in the Far East. He had swimmy black eyes, a brown complexion and inky black hair. He had a high-pitched laugh and exuded hints of his perverse interests. He overspent, was always in financial trouble, dunned his friends, did everything to excess, including drinking, and squandered his remarkable literary gifts. Publishers were not encouraged to advance money on books he neglected to write. His rakishness was the death of him, he invited criminals into his house and they tied him up and gagged him too tight.

The Pope-Hennessy brothers had a formidable mother, Dame Una Pope-Hennessy, a noted blue stocking. I never met her, but gossip suggests that neither of her boys would have dared to look at another woman while she was alive even if they had wanted to.

30 June

I met T S Eliot at tea with Violet Schiff. She told him that I wanted to be a writer and he said it was a very difficult career. He spoke the truth, but discouragingly. Some years later, Jock Murray suggested that Tom Eliot should decide whether or not he was to publish my book, *A Letter*. I asked for Violet's opinion. She replied: 'Don't agree, don't do it – Tom's never had anything nice to say about any living author.' For the record, it was John Betjeman who made up Jock's mind with his enthusiastic foreword.

Eliot looked to me more like a bank manager

than a poet (he had worked in a bank). He was very low-toned. He smoked cigarettes in a gloomy way. At the time he lived with an Oxford don, John Hayward, who was dying of MS. By all accounts he cheered up when he remarried. He was never flush with money, but his least serious work made posthumous millions via Andrew Lloyd-Webber's musical, *Cats*.

Belatedly, I sympathise with T S Eliot for having to meet me. No doubt he was sick of being expected to encourage would-be writers, and had learnt from experience to be non-committal. Years later I myself was bullied by an old friend to see an aspiring scribbler, son of a friend of my friend. I not only could not spare the time to see this youth, but also had no practical advice to offer, was sure that every writer has to work things out for himself, and nervous of treading on toes and giving offence. However, eventually I knuckled under and the aspirant accepted an invitation to come to tea. He was large and he was silent. As a result I talked more than I wanted to, and regretted the whole stupid business. The youth turned into a journalist and gave my popular book *Gentleman's Gentleman* a vengeful review.

Cyril Connolly's *Enemies of Promise* is a tragic book. Those enemies were too much for Cyril, who had seemed to be cut out to write more than a few patchy books. His editorship of *Horizon* was not the sort of achievement he had surely hoped for. Writers imperil their creative faculty by knowing too much about literature. They show they have run out of creative steam when they write about the art of writing.

I met E M Forster once. It was at Cambridge, we were having drinks before lunch with Patrick Wilkinson and his wife – I remember no other guests. He was a dingy little old man in a three-piece suit sitting in an armchair by the fire. He wore woolly bedroom slippers and never opened his mouth – signs of his genius?

Forster's book *Howards End* came in for a waggish criticism: 'Howards beginning is better than *Howards End*.'

Sacheverell Sitwell was more fun than pompous Osbert. When I met him he asked me: 'Have you written any good books lately?'

Hostesses cannot count on gratitude for the dinners and treats they dish out. Dickens mocked the Veneerings and Proust mocked the Verdurins for their generous entertainments. Nearly all the writers who skulked in comfort and safety at Garsington during World War I attacked their hostess, Lady Ottoline Morell, in their books. D H Lawrence, the most mixed-up of mixed-up kids, that hell of a genius, understood some things but misunderstood most, and thought his foul treatment of Lady Ottoline would not affect their friendship. He got the wife he deserved, Frieda, a German he-woman who was dead-set on making him and everybody else miserable.

Aldous Huxley was another snake in Lady Ottoline's grass – and, as some wit said in a different context, there was not a lot of grass.

The upper crust that accepted Laura Corrigan's bribes from Cartier to attend her functions jeered at her for being American and rich, and the guests of Lady Cunard also bit the hand that had fed them. The best of many jokes at the expense of Lady Colefax was that she lured people to her table by telling them they would meet the Unknown Soldier.

7 July

The late Donald Dewar has put the cat amongst the socialist pigeons by leaving two million pounds – he was supposed to be an ascetic puritan, undeviatingly red, but had invested in privatised utilities while in government and opposing their creation.

At a dinner party in Hong Kong a lady asked her Chinese neighbour: 'Do you ever eat brown rice?'

The gentleman replied: 'Brown rice is for poor people.'

'But brown rice is full of vitamins.'

'I get my vitamins in a bottle,' he said.

8 July

There is an eighth Age of Man, the Age of Indignity, and, medically speaking, I am in it.

* * *

Pills in bottles are a reminder that I rattle. I am grateful for, and embarrassed by, the largesse of my medical advisers. I call myself the Phantom of the Pharmacy. How on earth can my country afford me?

So-called tycoons, loveable or not, captains of industry, men of power, the big employers, the wealth creators, should be knelt down to or at least looked up to by poor folk and old folk and all beneficiaries of the Welfare State. Egalitarians are inclined to call them fat cats and parasites: where do they think the money lashed out on the NHS, and our innumerable benefits of one sort and another, come from?

The facts of the matter are that people are soon spoilt, they take gifts for granted, gratitude is a wasting asset, and privileges turn into rights.

12 July

Beware of doctors with bad secretarial back-up!

The bandwagon rolls towards the legalisation of cannabis. I believe Baudelaire rather than Lib-Labs. Baudelaire described his own experience in *Les Paradis Artificiels*. He said that cannabis affects and eventually destroys the will, the will-power that enables us to perform our existential duties. Cannabis causes physical and mental listlessness, and Baudelaire bitterly regretted that he became its slave.

14 July

List of foibles and faults that affect sober intelligent persons in their latter years:
1. Unstoppable verbosity;
2. A determination to be the centre of attention, relentless drive for selfish ends, sulking if crossed;
3. Megalomania that stops just short of madness, characterised by boasting, no interest in anyone else's existence, and extreme irritability;
4. Religious mania, which persuades some people to think they have a private line to God and need to obey none of the laws laid down in the Holy Bible or the rules of social life;
5. Irrational attitude to money, penny-pinching in well-heeled ladies who are convinced they are ruined, while men squirm on the horns of a dilemma – will they die before they have enjoyed spending their capital, or will they live after they have spent it?
6. Fund-raising *sans frontières*, that is with no holds barred, a substitute for the give and take, or take and give, of the competitive sexual exchanges of yore;
7. Foolhardiness, exhibited by blind drivers of ninety, and by superannuated yachtsmen, potholers, mountaineers and parachutists who have to be rescued by brave men at great risk.

15 July

No public sympathy in the country for policemen who kill people threatening to kill them and others, and no sympathy for policemen who do not stop madmen and murderers killing people: that is democracy in action, and why leadership differs from it.

18 July

Yesterday I was informed of the results of the tests I have been undergoing. Thank God, they were okay. Tomorrow we will be told how G's treatment is or is not working. Our hearts go out to everyone else waiting for the results of tests, and to everyone who has waited.

A scene sticks in my memory. At the hospital, in the changing room to which I returned after my tests, a young woman sat in one of the chairs, bowing her head low over a magazine. She wore another of the white dressing-gowns of towelling, and was obviously about to be summoned for an x-ray examination of some kind. She did not look up when I entered the room, she remained in the same rigidly bowed and rather unnatural position. I did not believe she was reading the magazine, and, rightly or wrongly, imagined she was afraid and sorrowful. She was very young, perhaps thirty, and I was so sorry for her.

19 July

G's treatment is working, but slowly. She rises above it.

21 July

Reverting once more to the effects of seniority on certain citizens, I refer to the increasingly common case of the hyperactive pensioner. Nowadays, old people sign on for package tours offering dawn starts to sight-seeing expeditions, a fortnight of bus rides, walking, swimming, games, evenings of seven-course dinners, then dancing into the small hours. Night flights on chartered aeroplanes to faraway places seem to deter nobody over sixty-five. In Eventide Homes, single old men have to lock their doors at night against harassment by their lusty female counterparts. The coupling of the ancients of days is now possible with the aid of science and no doubt leads to further expenditure of effort.

Excess on top of excesses, as usual, is reserved for 'higher' society. No debutante is so social as the bejewelled biddy who breaks and enters into every party. Cocktails here, dinner there, a ball until you are swept out with the detritus, luncheon somewhere else on the next day, and anything but a quiet evening at home – these are the preferred conditions of existence for unreconstructed flibbertigibbets. Tiredness is no excuse, satiety is simply not on the menu, ill health alters nothing, distance is no bar to a good time, 'pace' is the best of last words – and people who disagree are spoilsports.

22 July

Belas Knap and Soldier's Grave are prehistoric burial barrows located in the Cotswolds. Clifford Chambers is a Cotswold village, and Whispering Knights is the remains of a circle of stones. Egypt Mills at Nailsworth made cloth. Bliss Gate is near the Wyre Forest. Sweet surprising English names, not yet 'modernised'.

Story entitled *The Poor Philanthropist*: John was honest and poor for the first half of his life. He had been an orphan at twenty and was now pushing thirty-one, he stacked the shelves in a supermarket, dwelt in a remote lodging house, ate food past its sell-by date and rejected the idea of a wife whom he could not support. But then he had a flutter on the Lottery and won millions. He married Jane, a check-out girl aged forty, who was nicknamed Plain Jane. He liked her because she was as disadvantaged as he had been, and he was proud to wave his magic wand over her destiny. They bought a house in town and another in the country. She went shopping, he gave some of his money away or tried to. His relations, who had not been kind to him when he was poor, were nasty to him because he was rich. His gifts were either mingy and mean or distributed unfairly, they said, and their thanks were qualified by envy. He gave money to his friends, and they took umbrage: they could manage quite well without his patronage, and some made it clear that they were not for sale. Public charities were different in that they held out hot hands for more and still more, but caused suspicions to cross his mind: why did charities spend so much of the money on glossy brochures, extravagant adverts and administration? Further disillusionment was in store for him. Plain Jane sued him for divorce and the law enabled her to get away with half his remaining capital. Honest John told everybody that he had no money left, which was not completely true. But he almost felt sorry for himself and was inclined to mutter under his breath, 'Poor me!'

23 July

A brief history of my acquaintanceship with female beauty is comparable to a minefield. I shall start with the harmless past and end at a safe distance from the present. David Cecil told me he treasured memories of my mother in a filmy ball-dress of butterfly blue, and of his own sister Mary, later Duchess of Devonshire, waltzing at a ball: he commented on their airs of distinction and high spirits as well as their beautiful youth, and considered that they were the stars of his generation. He was also an admirer of Diana Cooper, who once upon a time must have deserved the praise lavished on her looks. But when I knew Diana, from the late fifties onwards, I could not admire that pale chilly countenance and deadpan expression. Vita Sackville-West as debutante was admired by my mother, who said she looked like a gipsy girl. Sad to think of Vita in the breeches and boots of her older age with her bucolic complexion, as it is to be reminded that my friend Cynthia Asquith, with not a trace of beauty, had formerly been one of the pair of 'moon goddesses', the other being Diana Cooper.

My Aunt Laura Lovat also lost her looks too early: in her youth she had deserved the nickname Lady Love-at-first-sight.

Joan Moore, the pianist, Countess of Drogheda, differed from the professional beauties, for she had other interests, her musicianship and career in concert halls, and her exhaustive reading and knowledge of literature. Her beauty, which no doubt cut both ways in relation to her life as an artist, was reinforced by her intelligence, and because it expressed the sympathetic warmth of her nature.

Beautiful womanhood does not necessarily denote a *femme fatale*. The fatal female has physical magnetism combined with a contrary and even perverse nature and a ruthless streak. An example was Patricia Douglas, later de Bendern, then Hornak, a relation of Oscar Wilde's undoing, Lord Alfred Douglas. Pat was not even very pretty, she had and retained into middle age a school-girlish face and figure, yet she was unusually and perhaps involuntarily seductive.

I dare to say no more.

Lord Alfred Douglas lived and died in Brighton. In his latter years he accepted an invitation to lunch with some friends, who all agreed not to mention the scandal of his youth. But the relevant name slipped out, Lord Alfred heard it, and announced in a loud voice: 'I used to be thick with Oscar Wilde.'

24 July

The *homme fatal* also exists. It might be that a *femme fatale* is only subjugated by an *homme fatal*; but in my view such poetic justice is unlikely. The men and women referred to either have a special gift for identifying willing fatalities, or their attractions are reserved for masochists. I cannot imagine two fatal people getting together.

Don Juan is not always *fatal.* Womanisers can be bad or relatively good for women.

31 July

Putting to bed *Tales of Love and War* – meaning, that I have chosen the better of two roughs of the dust jacket, checked that my corrections of the proofs have been corrected, and given the text one last reading.

In the world of my work there are two warning lights. One stops me rewriting what I have written. I may know it is faulty, but, at the same time, that I can do no better, and if I fiddle with it I shall compound old faults and introduce new ones. The second light comes on when I am correcting work – it is the signal of satiety.

It tells me I have done enough and had enough of proof-reading or whatever, and must call a halt and give up.

What an eye-opener it was for me when Leslie Hartley confessed that he did not revise his work! That was before I had heard of the weird ways in which some books get written. Ghosts lurk in many a bookshelf, and the fingerprints of editors are left on books. How much of Ian Fleming's work was done by William Plomer, poet and his publisher? Is it true that large parts of Bertolt Brecht's plays were written by the actress/actresses who would act in them? Sarah Bernhardt undoubtedly wrote most of the surviving version of Dumas' *La Dame aux Camélias*. Literary wives, literary secretaries, are often handed first drafts of books of which the authors wash their hands – Ursula Codrington, who typed for Leslie Hartley, chose and supplied 'his' adjectives.

Back to the subject of beauty: at a ball at the start of a London 'season' of long ago somebody asked Sir Edward Marsh, Winston Churchill's unwed private secretary, 'Well, Eddie, who are the beauties this year?' to which Sir Edward replied, 'I think he's rather beautiful.'

4 August

In art, the shocking card has now been played too often. Modernism equals reheated sensationalism. Sexual perversion is yesterday's mashed potato.

Iconoclasm is just pulling a long nose at your superiors. The look-at-me specialists are ten a penny. Nihilism has been seen to mean what it says – nothing. The way forward? Read Hamlet's speech to the players.

5 August

Some years ago Sir Martyn Beckett MC asked John Grigg to give the address at his funeral. John agreed, and the other day went to visit Martyn in hospital where he lay terminally ill. Martyn greeted John thus: 'You're on!'

6 August

Thetis Blacker, the painter and our friend, sent me a mail order catalogue issued by OKA which markets household furnishings. It arrived by post, and she referred me to page 28, an illustration of a small standing bookcase, and to one of the books filling the shelves – my book *Gentleman's Gentleman* in its first edition. What a delightful start to the morning! Perhaps only Thetis would have thought of studying that catalogue with a magnifying glass, spotting one out of thirty or forty books, and passing on the result of her research to gratify an old author.

8 August

That delightful subject, female beauty: my negative suggestion would be that it is recognisable only by being impossible to describe. Women blessed or cursed with it are also indescribable because they operate on a level different from the rest of us – different laws, values, preoccupations, aims, fears and practicalities govern their existence.

The career of Helen of Troy, whose face launched the thousand ships bearing soldiers to fight the Trojan War, is anti-climactic. She began by marrying Menelaus, left her husband for Paris, when Paris was slain in 'her' war she married his brother Deiphobus, then had him killed by her first husband Menelaus, with whom she settled down and lived quietly in the country until death carried her off.

9 August

I am mistaken for somebody else with Shakespearean regularity. My worst case occurred at Glyndebourne a few years ago. A young woman approached and enfolded me in an unsolicited embrace, saying how wonderful it was to see me after so long. I made the mistake of signifying agreement, and the following conversation ensued.
'Oh we did have such fun in the old days!'
'We did indeed!'
'I'll never forget the tennis matches.'
'Same here.'
'Is your mother still alive?'
'I'm afraid not.'
'What a shame! I never will forget her underarm serve, nor her home-made lemonade.'
'Did she make lemonade?' I queried, cudgelling my brains as to whom I was talking.
'She certainly did – fancy you forgetting that!

But how are you?' She regarded me with some anxiety, clearly thinking I was going Alzheimer's way. 'Are you all right?'

'I'm fine, and I don't need to ask how you are, I can see you're flourishing.'

'Thank you. I'm married and the mother of two.'

'Well done!'

'Are you married?'

'I am.'

'Oh do introduce me to your wife!'

'I can't – she's not with me at the moment – I don't know where she is.'

A shadow flitted across the face of my interlocutor – my answer had been on the hysterical side, I suppose, since I did not know her name and could not have introduced her.

'Aren't we lucky to be at Glyndebourne this evening?' she inquired with traces of doubt.

'Aren't we just!'

'Did you come all the way from Hampshire? You are still living in the ancient family pile, aren't you?'

'Hampshire?' I ventured to say. 'No, I've never lived in Hampshire, I was brought up in Gloucestershire.'

'Who are you then?'

I told her.

'Well, really!' she exclaimed and stalked off in high dudgeon.

11 August

In my youth I enjoyed doing lots of things which I now struggle to refrain from telling young people not to do.

At last I have come across a book that I cannot believe I will ever want to read: Duncan, I K, *A Guide to the Study of Lichens* (T Buncle, Arbroath, 1959).

12 August

Sunday, the Sabbath, the day of rest, and as usual I wish I had not read my newspaper.
   Tomorrow we leave for our week of summer holiday, and hope it will cheer but not inebriate, as the Scots say about tea.

21 August

Happy children beside the sea, happy families by the English sea, charm, amuse and revive hope. The inevitable 'but' refers to all the obesity on view. It was tragic to see those fat and fated young persons waddling to and from the ice cream shop.

Read Harold Acton's *More Memories of an Aesthete* with enjoyment. I met him once after he had given a splendid lecture – I forget the subject, but not his delivery, which was urbane and amusing: as is his book.

* * *

Acton describes in detail a holiday he spent with his friend Evelyn Waugh. It reveals in terms not altogether friendly Waugh's behaviour, the contrariness, the brutishness replete with bullying, the half-crazed impersonation of an eighteenth century aristo by the son of a middle-class twentieth century publisher. Genius, especially the literary sort, is apt to go with bad character and unpleasant personality, often with madness too. Waugh proved his genius with *Brideshead Revisited*.

24 August

Something called The Artwave takes place in Lewes this evening. It seems to be partly rustic carnival and partly late night shopping. No doubt it will all end in boozing.

26 August

Reading Anthony Powell's *The Kindly Ones*, part of his *Music of Time* series of novels. His prose reminds me of a steamroller cracking nuts; yet it instils a sense of security because of its good manners and implied promise that nothing too shocking is in store for the reader. I met the Powells once – they were very nice. He fagged for David Cecil at Eton (ran David's errands and toasted his muffins for tea), and they kept up in later life. David enjoyed Anthony's company more than his books, although he went in fear of the curries with which the Powells were apt to regale their guests. At my meeting with them,

Anthony said he had seemed to spend his days of work at *The Times Literary Supplement* packing up books to be sent to me to review.

27 August

In the Glyndebourne Festival just ended, my favourite opera was Janacek's *The Makropulos Case*. I loathed it when I first heard it, and other performances simply went over my head. But I learned to love it, and to love more and more the music, especially the overture and the final ten or fifteen minutes. Moreover, now, the libretto makes sense to me, and I see why Janacek chose to set it to music.

28 August

I quote from memory Harold Acton who was quoting a Chinese sage: 'Happiness is only possible by exclusive absorption in art.' But how hard it is to try to live exclusively for art!

29 August

Anthony Powell has invented a whole social system which, in literary terms, is comparable to Burke's *Peerage, Baronetage and Knightage* coupled with *Who's Who*. Less flatteringly, it is like those genealogical pages which we do not understand and tend to skip at the beginning of old-time fiction. Another comparison springs to mind: when he launches into yet another disquisition about heredity, relationships, and who was or had been or hoped to be married to whom, and children legitimate and illegitimate and cousins and halves and steps, I am reminded of a schoolmaster of mine who knew the national railway time-table by heart and loved to be asked how one could travel from Llandudno to Perth via Bognor Regis.

Here are words that I find difficult to spell: stye (in the eye – rarely sty); riveting; coquettish; eighth; coypus (S. American rodents); cocoon; coccyx (bone at base of spine); plied (past tense of ply); barre (rail used by ballet dancers); zoophyte (animal that looks like a plant); viscountcy; tappet (part of combustion engine); sapphire; lay-bys; irreplaceable.

31 August

To London yesterday to lunch with John and Patsy Grigg: he is in his seventy-eighth year and said that he could just about see the end of the fourth hefty volume of his life of Lloyd George – and there is yet another volume to come.

1 September

The fair sex should stop me feeling that I ought to write a sequel to *Cautionary Tales for Women*. Consider Agnes, a career-girl, a banker on the way up, efficient and not ugly, who fell in love with Martin, an accountant, mathematically strong but rather a wimp in other respects. She was twenty-six, he was twenty-four; she had loved no other man as she loved Martin from the word go; he was taken aback and perturbed by the passion he had inspired. But at the Christmas 'office' party, encouraged by John Barleycorn, he allowed himself to be seduced – ironically, in the bank vault reserved for Security Deposits. Agnes was soon happy to find herself pregnant, and, taking it for granted that the father of her child would do the honourable thing, hurried to tell him the good news. With outpourings of gratitude, with promises that she would take care of everything, himself not least, and with her vision of their perfect little family unit, she swept him to the altar. And she was as good as her word: she bore him two healthy children, ran a comfortable home, arranged her life so that she could continue to work at the bank and contribute a second income to family funds, denied her husband nothing, and was not forgiven by her friends for having such an enviable marriage. Martin's announcement that he was in love with someone else hit her hard. But she recovered some sort of composure and discussed the matter sympathetically. She referred to mid-life crises. She said she would not object to a spot of discreet adultery. She let him talk about his mistress, a twenty-year-old aspiring model called Polly. She also did her rather shocking best to exhaust him sexually. He then told her that Polly was going to study modelling and acting in America for six months, and when she returned he intended to set divorce proceedings in train. He would stay put for that period, he continued, and continue to cohabit, especially as he had new social responsibilities connected with his work and would require Agnes' assistance. She agreed, she submitted, she was sure he would change his mind. In the ensuing months Agnes worked her fingers to the bone for Martin – and not only her fingers, for they still slept in the marital bed. She cooked delicious dinners in order to advance his career, and ate dinners that she often found unpalatable to please him. She was ready for anything he suggested, never moody, never challenging. And she never asked what had become of his intentions – he could not be so horrible as to spurn her after all, she imagined. But one day he asked her to help him to pack his things. What had he said, what did he mean? She laughed in disbelief, told him he could not do it, prophesied that if he did he would rue the day, and so on. Hoping to frighten him somehow, she actually did do some of his packing. He walked out on her with his suitcases, some of which she carried to his car, and her optimistic suggestion when he pecked her cheek in response to her clinging hug, 'See you soon', was not quite the end of the story. They divorced. Polly married a different man. Martin's second marriage was to a different woman. Agnes was left alone to reflect that love as one-sided as hers is a mistake.

2 September

Passion and lust are natural. Passion and lust know no boundaries. Without religion and fear of the fires of hell, passion and lust can and do become criminal.

* * *

Tales of Love and War is scheduled for publication in the second half of January 2002, a time when, I was once encouraged incorrectly, so few books get published that critics are willing to review the telephone directory.

4 September

Feminism – is it proactive flirting and a short cut to becoming a damsel in distress? The fair sex is also the weaker one, and muscles do not believe in equality. Very few women are able to overpower their husbands or lovers – physically, I mean. Women of a certain age with children, living in poor circumstances, have no realistic alternative to getting beaten up by their worse halves. Cruel men can frighten lots of women into not leaving them. Girls, beware! Love does not have to be, it should not be, a white-knuckle ride. Take cross references if possible before you 'behave like a man', commit yourself or agree to marry. Sex, exclusive sex, is no substitute for sympathy, comprehensive sympathy; and no sex, or too little, is another danger signal.

The excuses of men echo down the years. Women's accounts of men's violence are always 'grossly exaggerated'. Women 'bruise themselves', are 'frightful whingers', are 'romancers, neurotics, psychological cases, liars, out to make trouble, bloodsuckers and bitches'. Men claim they were 'only teasing', that their wretched partners 'have no sense of humour', that they themselves are actually the victims of the relationship and are scared stiff of frail creatures with black eyes and broken bones. How are you to react to those solemn promises that offenders 'did not mean it ... had not known it would be taken so hard ... would never do it again ... would be different, good, kind, gentle, sweet in future,' and the accompanying pleas and prayers to be given a second or a last chance, to be reinstated in order to create more misery? Are you strong enough to say 'No, thanks – forget it – get lost – goodbye'?

Do not imagine that such dilemmas, such disasters, happen only to other people, you well-brought-up middle class girl with hopes and ideals! Wife-beaters abound. Everywhere sadists either have sought out or are seeking masochists. I know popular members of the establishment whose recreation is to torment and torture their wives.

7 September

Byron's Diary beckons. *The Third Time* tempted me to interrupt my first journal, *Marking Time*. I wonder if history is repeating itself. The attractions of the Byron book would be the mystery and the deception.

A new game could rival Happy Families – it would be called Unsuitable Appointments and also be played with cards – the method of play undecided as yet. For example, in my lifetime in the Kingdom that was United, we have elected Scotsmen to govern England and a terrorist to educate children in Ireland. Our Arts Council is run by a gentleman also responsible for service stations on motorways. We have republicans swearing allegiance to our Queen, egalitarians queueing up to be lordships and ladyships, money-mad socialists, and pacifists in charge of armies. Not long ago a curmudgeon who had hurt the feelings of most of his compatriots was put in charge of race relations. We have sportsmen who are renowned more for their unsportsmanlike behaviour than their skill. And the personage summoned to organise entertainment in Tony Blair's Dome was a lawyer.

8 September

The new Lewes library will not be built. The plan has been scrapped because local government is four million pounds poorer than it should have been. We are not meant to dish out blame just yet. The Conservatives have not run the Town or County Councils for several years.

9 September

I am going to set aside my journal for the time being, and see if I can squeeze a short book out of my idea for *Byron's Diary*.

7 November

Between the last entry and this one, an example of man's inhumanity, ranking with the great horrors of history, has occurred. On September 11, in an attack of undeclared war, several thousand civilians of mixed nationalities were killed in minutes. The murders were committed in the name of the Muslim religion. So far the international leaders of the Muslim community have not publicly disassociated themselves from the act.

My lifetime was overshadowed by the cruelty of marxism and nazism in action, and I foresee my life ending in the course of another long, horrible and ultimately pointless period of conflict.

I think of the saying of an unsophisticated friend of ours: the best we can do at such times, at all times, is to keep our own little corners bright.

Incidentally, I have written the first draft of *Byron's Diary* in thirty-eight days for better or worse.

12 November

A Sussex gardener spoke to us of the Americans having trouble with 'that there Andrex' – he meant anthrax, not lavatory paper.

My second draft of *Byron's Diary* is now complete. The third and last will not take long. Writing seems easier after Gerard Noel's praise of my *Collected Works* in the *Catholic Herald*.

13 November

Cecil Beaton continued to bring out diaries long after he should have stopped. He lent my sister

June the diary that described his 'love affair' with Greta Garbo – he asked her to read it and tell him if he could or should publish it. June was uncertain and passed it on to me. My verdict was that of course he should not publish but that of course he would – and he did. The diary showed that he courted Garbo more for publicity purposes than for love, and what a go-getter he was.

Jim Lees-Milne's amusing and reckless diaries are still being published posthumously. I suspect that he is ill-served by his executors and editors. On the other hand the more recent ones seem to warn women against marriages of his type, which resembled Harold and Vita's. Alvilde was the daughter of a general, but even she with her militant disposition complained of Jim's extra-marital activities. One day both Lees-Milnes were invited to lunch somewhere. Jim chucked, Alvilde went alone. When she arrived, her hostess said how sorry she was that Jim was otherwise engaged with his nephew. To which Alvilde replied: 'They're always his nephews.'

20 November

I have finished *Byron's Diary*. It must be about the twenty-fifth book of mine, including the Harlequin mini-books, that Diana Crook has typed faultlessly for me, correcting draft after draft. Her work has complemented mine in other ways – she is my archivist, and the archival system she invented has been approved and even copied by the British Library. Her comments on my texts have never been destructive, while her suggestions have always been wise and often improved my writings. She is my colleague, and I set great store by her opinions.

21 November

I have advance copies of *Tales of Love and War*. My friends at the Book Guild of Lewes have done an excellent job so far, but I wonder whether they can distribute it even as well as Constable did with other books of mine – that is to say, I do not expect to sell many copies.

24 November

A book which I shall not write could be amusing and would be topical – title: *Human Consistency – A Lost Cause*.

Here is an example: in the *Observer's Book of Wild Animals of the British Isles*, the revised edition published in 1958, the two expert authors open the entry on the fox with the following sentence: 'It is safe to say that ... the fox would have been placed long ago on the list of extinct British animals, but for its careful preservation by the various "hunts".' Now, almost fifty years later, the sentimentalists and the inverted snobs want to outlaw hunting with dogs – they object to the 'cruelty' of the sport of 'hunting'. No doubt the politics of ignorance will get its law on to the Statute Book. As a result the anti-hunting brigade will kill off many highly developed breeds of hounds, fox, stag, otter hounds, 'natural' as distinct from racing greyhounds, beagles and so on, will decimate the horse population and probably cause the fox's extinction.

26 November

Less than a month to go until the shortest day of the year, 21 December, after which days lengthen and spring comes in.

27 November

True diaries are records of events. True diarists are recorders, they are not led on by the discoveries, surprises and excitement of creative writing unless they are liars.

I feel a bit flat in a literary sense after tearing through *Byron's Diary*. I used to write slowly, now I have joined the speed merchants. I am amazed by the number of books I have written – after my first I was almost convinced that I would never write another.

The genesis of *War and Peace* occupied thirteen years, from 1856 to 1869. Tolstoy claimed that he put his whole heart and soul into his book – a proceeding Byron warned against, advising writers always to hold something back and keep a secret or two. Byron might have been proved right, for in my opinion Tolstoy never recovered mentally from the huge creative effort. I am not comparing myself with Tolstoy, far from it, but do know that keeping control of long books is terribly difficult and a terrible strain: computers may seem to be a solution, but in fact beget a whole range of new problems. Tolstoy himself thought it had been a bad idea to embark on *Anna Karenina*, another heavy tome, immediately after *War and Peace*. He loathed it, got stuck in the middle, had to force himself to complete it, and found fault with it to his dying day. Parts of *Resurrection* written in his old age are excellent, so are the stories of his even older age, but the two marathons, *War and Peace* and *Anna Karenina*, seem to have robbed him of common sense and compassion for persons, if not for people.

Dostoevsky's books show genius and often his epilepsy and mental instability as well. *Crime and Punishment* is disturbing not only because it is an ingenious murder story; and *The Brothers Karamazov* casts a sinister and unhealthy spell. One of the many divisions by which humanity in general and readers in particular can be described is that some people are born to love Tolstoy's 'straightforward' books and others to prefer Dostoevsky's 'psychological' ones.

1 December

In receipt of the umpteenth piece of evidence attesting to the unfailing capacity of members of my extended family, even the most distant of my relations, to live beyond their means.

2 December

My grandfather on my father's side went bust, my great-grandfather on my mother's side ditto – he also committed suicide. My father died aged fifty-five in financial distress. One cousin of his had to 'cut down a tree in order to buy a bottle of gin', as the family put it, and he and another cousin handed over to their heirs estates that were bankrupt. The widow of yet another cousin of my father's generation inherited a fortune and ran through it, and her daughter frittered away her own fortune in the course of a short life.

My brother papered the walls of a dining-room in one house he lived in with prints of the grander residences our forebears had built, inherited, dwelt in, and been forced to sell, including Apethorpe in Northamptonshire and Mereworth Castle in Kent.

5 December

What are these: Ancient Wife, Cock Paddle, Colin, Father Lasher, Longnose, Miller's Dog, Sweet Lips? Answer: sea creatures.

Harold Pinter has publicly tried to moderate his speech urging people to attack America delivered a day or two before the Muslim extremists did so. The speech was meant to thank an Italian University for presenting him with an award of some description.

6 December

My friend Anne Tree, upon whom part of the perennial political mantle worn by the Cecil family, her maternal forebears, seems to have fallen, said yesterday that our country was now out of control. I agree, and hope we may be proved wrong.

I have tried for years to ignore reviews of my books, not always successfully. Reviewers seldom review my work nowadays – I am old, no longer news, and have steered clear of the literary rat race in London. Appreciative notices are nice nonetheless, as nice as the other sort are nasty and somehow unforgettable.

7 December

The best and most intelligent English review I have received was of *Money Matters*, written by Adam An-tAthair-Síoraí and published in *Icarus*, the journal of Mensa. The best and most intelligent review of my work in general and my *Collected Works* in particular was written by the author and editor Gerard Noel and appeared in *The Catholic Herald*. Both *Money Matters* and my *Collected Works* were ignored by the 'national' newspapers.

8 December

I see no ships, only hardships. – Cockney saying.

9 December

G approves in the main of *Byron's Diary* – which is most satisfactory for me.

Beautiful cold weather, not comfortable for people with bad circulations.

10 December

Yesterday the Turner Prize was awarded to an empty room with lights that go on and off at five second intervals – the judges were also intentionally or unintentionally making a comment on Philistia, the Great Britain of yore. Another such comment was their choice of prize-giver, the American pop and film star Madonna, who in a short speech upset millions of people watching on TV. I repeat that nothing succeeds like offence.

With thanks to our friend and neighbour Tony Shephard, here are a few uncommon examples of Cockney rhyming slang: Jeremiah = fire; Gawd forbids = kids; Cain and Abel = table; daft and barmy = army; royal soup and gravy = navy; frog and toad = road; Donald Duck = luck; taters in the mould = cold; Piccadilly Percys = mercies; Jim Skinner = dinner; Forsyte Saga = lager; jam tart = heart.

Reading *The Faustian Bargain* by Jonathan Petropoulos, the story of the German artists and middlemen of the arts who lent their support to the nazi regime. Could they have done otherwise? I wish that many had not made fortunes, got off scot-free after the war, and hung on to their money.

11 December

Books I just want to look at, and maybe read, I borrow from David Jarman's membership library located a hundred and fifty yards from our home. It occupies approximately two rooms, financially must hang on a shoestring, and is an admirable enterprise really run on a combination of David's charm, taste and reassuring love of books.

A grim statistic, culled from the Bookseller publication *Who Owns Whom, 1998*: Random Century, the English subsidiary of Random House USA, owned at the time twenty-two different publishing imprints. Since 1998, the German group Bertelsmann has bought Random Century, therefore its eleven imprints (1998 tally) have to be added to Random Century's twenty-two – Bertelsmann must now own thirty-three of the better-known imprints operating as British publishers. What percentage of the whole publishing industry in this country does that add up to? Is it almost a monopoly? No question that it is a monolithic bureaucracy – not a very clever development, when everybody who knows anything about the literary life is convinced that only individuals, who love the printed word and have a nose for talent and quality, have ever been good at publishing.

12 December

We are feeding our garden birds in this cold weather. They are not active while it is dark – owls and nightjars must be the exceptions proving the rule that most birds cannot see to fly and to land on twigs until the sun has risen. Avian meal-times seem to be as strict as they were in middle class Victorian households – eating at anti-social hours is not always the done thing. Starlings have muscled in on the food we provide for smaller birds, and now a grey squirrel is bagging the biggest share – the bird world is not so different from ours.

13 December

The murderer of six-year-old 'Mary Sunshine' has been condemned to spend his whole life in prison – he is a pervert who sexually assaulted and killed a little girl, and, if ever given the chance, would be expected to strike again.

For the Sunshine family, the private tragedy grinds on; nationally, the comedy begins. The judge has no power to imprison Cain, the murderer, until he dies – he merely makes a recommendation to the Government that Cain should never be released. Therefore Home Secretaries in the plural are going to have to decide whether or not to keep Cain in prison after he has served his life sentence of a decade or so. If no liberal Home Secretary sets Cain free, he will join five or six other monsters who have become virtually political prisoners – I know of no law of lifelong imprisonment at the disposal of the judiciary. Everybody wants to sweep Cain and other murderers under the carpet, but nobody wants to pay for their comfortable living conditions until they die. There is an extraordinary conspiracy to censor the words that begin with the letters C and P. You can curse and swear to your heart's content on the stage, you can turn plays, films and TV linguistically into a barrackroom, you can spew out sedition publicly and blaspheme to your heart's content, but it is not done to say even in an undertone 'capital punishment'. I not only do say or rather write those words here, but I also challenge the anti-death-penalty mob to tell me what is the point and the use of keeping Cain and his ilk alive and in cages like pets at enormous expense for ever. Please do not con me with the story that you are against the shedding of blood, because you are a vegan and a pacifist: do you never wear leather, and refuse all medical assistance linked to the death of your fellow creatures when you are ill? Please remember, and own up, that you live on death, however strict your regime – carnivores and herbivores, birds and sea creatures, we all kill to eat, and hypocrisy cuts no ice with common sense. Cain should die – honesty would rule that it is good to be rid of bad rubbish – and in an overpopulated and increasingly violent world the death penalty will soon be forced on politics. It is already happening in an underhand way: Blair has pledged to hand over Bin Laden or any of his criminal gang, should they be apprehended by our troops, to the USA, which has promised to try them by drumhead courts and polish them off if necessary. Why are all our brave journalists, who criticise the defenceless Royal Family and the Church of England, so craven in respect of this issue? What are all the young Turks in the media, who can be rude to almost everyone, doing about the injustice of the law, which has freed murderers to kill children and others? Do-gooders believe we are all guilty of crime in general – I believe we are guilty of not making certain in the most cost-effective way that incorrigible murderers will lose their lives for taking life and can never do it again.

14 December

The successful redistributor of wealth is not a phoney political doctrine, but, practically and historically, sex. Cinderellas, Galateas, chorus girls transformed into duchesses, pretty faces that launch ships, and sundry other lucky sex-objects prove my point.

15 December

Times change, to coin a phrase: two young footballers, overpaid, under-educated, with records of violence and drunken brawling, are not sent to prison for helping nearly to kill an Asian youth, just as two hundred years ago upper-class hooligans would not have been imprisoned for a similar offence. Now the upper-class hooligan would be made an example of, while the thuggish entertainer is above the laws of the land.

16 December

The face of Osama bin Laden spills beans, I believe. His eyes are all very well, but his mouth is a disaster. It is the mouth of a clown, he has the blubbery lips of certain fish, they are joke lips of equal dimensions top and bottom made of rubber, and they contradict his eyes. He is dysplastic, he may well suffer from dysplasia in other parts of his anatomy, have a strong torso and rickety legs for all I know, or thin ankles and non-matching fat feet. *The Varieties of Human Physique* by W.H. Sheldon of Harvard University describes dysplasia thus: 'the aspect of disharmony between different regions of the same physique.' Sheldon's companion volume to the above, *Varieties of Human Temperament*, links physical and temperamental combinations and draws his various conclusions. Here are my own deductions from first-hand study of the dysplastic syndrome. The 'disharmony' accounts for personalities not fully integrated, for people who look sensitive but behave insensitively, or vice versa, for clever people with stupid streaks, or pacifists who fight for peace, or, in a catch-all couple of words, the inconsistent. Dysplasia seems to go with an inability to connect cause and effect – they are the charitable sadists and rough masochists, they are the loving husbands with downtrodden nervous wrecks of wives, or the loving wives who henpeck their hubbies, the fond and oppressive fathers, the sweet Oedipal sons, the phallic mothers, the vengeful daughters, and many others who carry their innate contradictions to measurable and even clinical lengths.

17 December

The whole story of a new novella, plus the title, came to me in the small hours of this morning during half an hour of wakefulness in bed. It will be called *Duress*, if it ever gets written.

Acquaintances and even my friends are apt to be unimaginative in respect of the life I lead and the lives of professional working people in general. Strangely, lovers of art seem to have the foggiest ideas of how art is created in practical terms – perhaps they also badgered Michelangelo to take time off from painting the ceiling of the Sistine Chapel and stay for the weekend and draw something nice in their Visitors Books. Social life is goodbye to art, and socialites can never or will never understand that the majority of artists and for that matter pros of every description, including craftsmen and artisans, need peace and quiet in which to prepare to do, and recover from, their work. A minority of exceptions burn their candles at both ends, and as a rule die of it.

Unusual artists with strong constitutions may be able to work and play almost simultaneously. But for Pushkin exiled to the depths of the country, Tolstoy snowed up at Yasnaya Polyana, Solzhenitsyn hiding from the secret police, Proust alone with his asthma in a cork-lined noiseless room, and for all the famous failures, for examples Vermeer and van Gogh, obscurity was the mother and father of their wonderful work.

An original expression of a widow's grief: 'I am sad that I no longer have to put down the seat of the lavatory.'

20 December

Sex without seriousness is nothing to write home about. True love on both sides, modesty on the female, confidence tempered with respect on the male, and shared awareness of the parameters of sin – these are the ingredients of the most powerful of aphrodisiacs in the human pharmacopoeia. Permissiveness and promiscuity equal wet blankets as well as sheets.

I now have two novellas in mind, *Duress* and *The Stepmother*. I hope to have the strength to write them, beginning perhaps after our holiday in February.

21 December

The shortest day of the year, praise be!

22 December

The Commissioners of Irish Lights bear a romantic name, but only look after lighthouses.

23 December

A few evenings ago we watched a programme on TV about Russian churches, their architecture, decoration, services and congregations. It was in all respects beautiful – snow lent further enchantment to the outdoor scenes, and we were spared a pretentious and distracting commentary. The members of the congregations were of both sexes and every age, and their faces as they watched and listened to the celebration of Christian rites seemed to glow with faith. I thought of the horrors they had lived through, of the seventy years of the communist experiment in Russia, of the blood, tears, bereavements, grief of their last century which was worse than ours, and gained understanding of their joy to be free to worship a deity who offered them not despotism, but consolation and hope.

Very bright cold weather continues – I await global warming in vain.

24 December

Regrettably, Scrooge-like feelings about children of all ages who do not thank for Christmas presents.

John Grigg extremely ill. He has been my friend for sixty years. A brilliant man, and a good one – rare combination! He is blessed with the happiest of marriages.

26 December

A peaceful Christmas Day – counted my blessings – worried about those less lucky – in the evening Sky TV showed a fine Italian production of Verdi's *Falstaff* – such a relief to see a great opera not defaced by the cheeky midgets who peddle 'contemporary' versions and 'relevance'.

Falstaff was first staged in 1893. Verdi was then eighty, according to my calculations, so must have been writing his last opera in his later seventies. The work sparkles with vivacity, humour, compassion and gentle morality, and has not only delighted audiences for more than a century, it also offers a glimmer of hope to septuagenarian practitioners of other arts, the writer of this diary, for example.

27 December

The other day I said to G, 'This year has been awful, so violent and sad – I'll be glad to see the back of it,' and G replied, 'You say that every year.'

28 December

Someone's theory is that the occupational hazard of the English upper class is melancholia. If true, that would explain the widespread weakness for the bottle of that class of person.

But drunkenness is more egalitarian than any radical philosophy or revolutionary action. It may be the second great leveller, poverty being the first.

How can poorer people afford to get drunk? How can richer people – a couple of alcoholics can drink up to twenty thousand pounds p.a., and much more if they are hospitable?

It is a mistake to judge alcoholics by the common or garden criteria. They have renounced 'normality' knowingly or unknowingly, they have left happiness and health far behind, and seek nothing but the relief of the next drink and the bitter joy of a loss of control of their lives.

29 December

Snow fell overnight, we awoke to a white world.

We have been discussing the phenomenon of J K Rowling, the girl who has written the Harry Potter books which have sold almost as well as the Bible. I saw her for a moment on TV and liked her, and G saw her for longer and thought she was a genuine vocational writer. She is now famous for ever and rich beyond the dreams of avarice; but more by accident than design, for she could not have aimed to make so stupendous a success and confine herself in a gilded literary cage. No book of hers not about Harry Potter will please her fans. A different sort of book will be meat to all the hungry carnivores of Grub Street, the critics and journalists, the poor hacks, the competitive female authors, the miffed publishers, the envious agents, the big battalions massed behind the green flag of jealousy. Any difference from the Harry Potter books will disappoint thousands of millions – not an inspiring prospect for a proper author always hoping to write a better book one day!

30 December

Last night a TV programme on John Betjeman in the *Reputations* series. It was pretty good, if somewhat pre-digested for his young admirers. Tastefully, it omitted much that I and other close friends know, while dropping occasional hints suggestive of a slightly different story: John's morning 'glass of champagne', for instance. G thought the programme failed to convey John's charm; but I was sorry that it left out his kindness to younger writers. Somebody expressed a hope that he would be judged by his work – a fitting epitaph for many fine artists.

Elizabeth Cavendish is too sensitive and sensible ever to discuss her relationship with John. Anyway, she has her niche in history, and deserves it.

31 December

One of Margaret Thatcher's brilliant insights was her talk of the 'courage of 3 a.m.' She meant it is braver to be brave in the small hours of the morning than at other times. Recently I have formed the bad habit of waking punctually at 3, therefore can quite agree with her. Worries seem to line up to assault you at that hour, adrenalin rushes in or out to repulse them, fear combined with exertion affects the rhythm of the heart, and only dawn promises rescue and relief. What would we do, what could we do, without morning?

George Christie of Glyndebourne has been made a Companion of Honour – one of the better things done by the government.

New Year's Day 2002

John Grigg died yesterday. His childhood home and ours were two miles distant across the fields. His mother Joan became my mother's friend when they nursed together in World War I. His grandmother, Lady Islington, mother of Joan, a beauty and a noted wit, was also my mother's friend. John's father, Ned Grigg, DSO, and with many other letters after his name, was a sweet benevolent grand old man in my memory, but never won over his mother-in-law Anne Islington, who insisted on calling him Grog. John was the eldest of three Grigg children and the same age as my brother David. Tormarton Court in Gloucestershire was a gracious manor house in a Cotswold style, and the Griggs lived there in considerable comfort. But the interests of the older Grigg generation were political and cultural, whereas my mother was more interested in the decorative arts and gardening, and my father in sport; and although my half-sister June made friends with John, there was no immediate meeting of minds between John and my brother. The latter took grave exception in his eleventh year or thereabouts to three harmless manifestations of John's personality: he said 'See you anon' instead of goodbye, he wore a French beret instead of an English cap, and he was discovered reading a leather-bound copy of Charlotte Brontë's *Villette*. The intolerance of the youth of David, who became a markedly tolerant adult, chose to think that John was attempting to pull intellectual rank by behaving so strangely by his standards, and John compounded his offences in David's eyes by speaking French fluently.

John and David were firm friends later on, but John's support of my literary leanings and my sympathy with his enthusiasms drew us closer together. I remember an early speech of his – it must have been just after the war. He was already a political activist, impatient to stir people up and change things, and he created a forum for lectures and discussion – it bore some blood-curdling name, the 1949 Club, I think, and met in the Church Hall at Tormarton. I went with my mother to one of his rousing efforts, in which he criticised the whole system of government of the country, made learned historical points, bashed into the Establishment, and called for a brand new better world. His audience consisted of his mother and mine and myself, a few other neighbourly gents and ladies in the front row, and otherwise the residents of the village of Tormarton, most of whom worked for the Griggs in various capacities. In response to the exhortations of the speaker, and when he finished and sat down, the cries that rang out took the form of either 'Hear hear, darling!' or in rich Gloucestershire accents, 'That's it, Master John ... You give it to them hot and strong, Master John ... Well said, Master John!'

In line with his attempt to revolutionise the clodhoppers of Tormarton and its environs, one day he invited me to write a piece that could be spoken or performed in the village church. He called for controversy, and I obliged to the extent of daring to produce a playlet about the wise and unwise virgins. John surprised me by thinking it too tame, I resisted his urgings to make it scandalous, and that was the end of that.

His notorious article about the monarchy was motivated by the spirit of his 1949 Club, that is by a somewhat blinkered high idealism and without malice. Taken in conjunction with his renunciation of the hereditary peerage of Altrincham conferred on his father, it put paid to his attempts to become a professional politician and launched his distinguished career as journalist, critic, historian and biographer.

John could be said to have been born with a silver spoon in his mouth, but he suffered with never a word of public complaint from lifelong ill health, from the eccentricity of his mother, and from problems created by his siblings. He was lucky to have been so intelligent and articulate, and such a fluent writer, but in my opinion he should not have done or had to do a lot of work unworthy of his talents. He was lucky to have been so charming, popular, hospitable, generous, but those delightful qualities are not especially conducive to literary composition. His only unqualified piece of luck was his marriage to Patsy and their family life.

He inherited some of the contentious inclinations of his forebears. Yet he was courtesy personified. In sixty-plus years of close friendship with him, I never knew or heard of him doing a mean or disreputable thing. He was at least as brave as his father, and his sense of humour was at least as keen and jolly as his grandmother Anne Islington's. He was the most modest of heroes, and I am honoured to remember that once upon a time, when we were both churning out books, we thought of calling ourselves the Gloucestershire Group.

2 January

Someone said to G: 'I don't like opera, I don't like opera singers, I don't like the way their mouths are always open.'

The euro is launched. Will pounds be replaced by euros? Blair promises a referendum on the issue. My guess is that the vote would go against it in the unlikely event of Blair keeping his promise. That the euro will find itself in trouble must be a sure thing. It may or may not be scrapped. If it survives, if Europe becomes one country, expect the process to be complete and successful in not less than a hundred and fifty years.

* * *

For sixteen days there has been no collection of refuse in Lewes.

5 January

Refuse was collected today, as Mr Pooter would write or should have written in his *Diary of a Nobody*.

Reading Nabokov on Gogol. I am impressed by both writers – I had known little about Nabokov, had only read *Lolita* which I thought rather awful, and although I much enjoyed Gogol's *Dead Souls* and *The Government Inspector* I had read nothing about Gogol himself. Nabokov in this blessedly and unfashionably short biography is excellent, loves his subject, communicates his enthusiasm for Gogol's writings, brings all to life with the grand sweep of his intelligence, impatient dismissal of trivialities, bold comparisons and muscular compassion. He presents us with two Gogols, an irresponsible crazy paranoid escapist and dreamer, and a soaring genius above and beyond mundane analysis, a surrealist who makes sense, a comic tragedian and tragic comedian almost tortured to death by doctors.

6 January

Our Prime Minister patronises the people of India by telling them that he is 'a force for good' and implying that they are not so. Where are his manners, where are his wits? No one can talk to the proud sophisticated satirical people of India like that. Blair will be laughed to scorn by Indians for dressing up like Nehru and not minding his own business.

11 January

PLR, the Public Lending Right, is an author's entitlement to a fee for each of his or her books borrowed from Public Libraries. This was a governmental concession fought for and won by Bridget Brophy and Maureen Duffy some decades ago. The present rate paid to an author for each loan is 2.67p – and the number of loans is calculated by averages and ready reckoning. If I should ever sink so low as to belong to a Trade Union, I would describe the 2.67p as 'derisive', and take strike action. Public Libraries were no doubt a good thing once upon a time, but these days they rip off authors and ruin the book trade. I would have earned a living wage for the last fifty years if my books had not been lent nationally to readers.

12 January

A further word of advice to young writers: do not give your books to members of your family, start by not giving them as you mean to go on, for your siblings and other relations will either not read them, or read and criticise them too harshly and for non-literary reasons. A gift of even one book to a family member can be a costly mistake, for you will then be expected to buy books for all the other members, who will reward you with still more lack of appreciation. In my opinion the best way to preserve your peace of mind, although your publisher's publicity people might not agree, is to disappear shortly before Publication Day and remain in limbo for a few months. After that sort of lapse of time your family will have forgotten your book – it probably never understood your literary leanings and will be pleased to think again that you are a bit of an idler and a parasite.

13 January

I quote from Nabokov's book about Gogol, the great Russian writer: 'When the critic Pogodin's wife died and the man was frantic with grief, this is what Gogol wrote to him: "Jesus Christ will help you to become a gentleman, which you are neither by education nor inclination – she [your wife] is speaking through me."'

14 January

Thinking of the range of ways to 'sandbag' a man and drag him to the altar. The woman who became the first wife of Sydney Schiff, Violet's husband, pretended to sleep or faint while they were together in some lonely wilderness and at the same time enabled him to make love to her. When she 'awoke' or recovered, or when the deed was done, she accused him of having taken advantage of her – to put it mildly – and exerted enough pressure to ring the wedding bells.

Sometimes the family and happy home life of a young man or woman can exercise the seductive influence that he or she lacks. Again, money can compensate for almost every physical, mental and social imperfection. Schoolgirls are told to be good if they are neither beautiful nor clever; but cynicism would advise them not to be too good if or when they want a man – availability, used with discretion, can overcome most male objections to romance.

The verb 'to sandbag' in the context above means to knock someone senseless. It was used in Edwardian times in the matrimonial connection because 'sandbagging' not only robs a potential husband of his senses, it has the added advantage of leaving no mark on the victim.

Sydney Schiff's *nom de plume* was Stephen Hudson. He tells the tale of his first marriage in his series of autobiographical novels, *A True Story*, which fell by the wayside long ago. He also translated *Time Regained*, the last volume of his friend Proust's masterpiece.

Violet, wife of Sydney Schiff/Stephen Hudson, was my friend when she was in her eighties and I was in my twenties. The friends of my youth nearly all died in the distant past. The names of those who first encouraged me to follow the star of letters are like the roll-call of the fallen after the battle of Agincourt in Shakespeare's *Henry V*: Dorian Williams, Mr Chilcot, J D Upcott, A R D Watkins, schoolmasters; Patrick Wilkinson, Cambridge academic; John Wyse, actor. My father died before I had heard the call to be a writer, and my mother was tolerant and supportive of my unremunerative literary beginnings. As for my parents-in-law, my work is deeply indebted to them for providing me with G. G's mother Juliet and father Jock Swire raised four outstanding children, and have had equally remarkable grandchildren. Jock Swire brought hope to Hong Kong after its wartime occupation by the Japanese and played a leading part in the drama of its revival, survival and success against all the odds.

16 January

Bullies in state schools are now to be taught elsewhere and stigmatised for life – a cruel punishment devised by liberals who will not teach a child a lesson by physical chastisement followed by forgiveness.

22 January

Publication Day for *Tales of Love and War.*

23 January

An impressive, long yet concise, and appreciative letter from our friend Pamela Wedgwood, *nom de plume* Pamela Tudor-Craig, about *Tales of Love and War.* She makes an interesting point re the great losses of marriageable men during World War I: as a result women outnumbered the opposite sex by such a large percentage that they were almost forced into the arms of husbands old enough to be their fathers – she quotes the example of her own mother.

24 January

The Book Guild has measured up to my expectations. The majority of London publishers should come to Lewes to learn how to do their jobs properly. Amazing that, after my half a century of professional authorship, I should find a publishing company providing the highest level of service to its authors within ten minutes walk of my home!

This description of a good sleeper was new to me: 'She could sleep on a clothes line.'

25 January

I quote from *A Need to Testify* by Iris Origo: 'Lytton Strachey ... considered biography "the most delicate and humane of all branches of the art of writing".' Biography is all very well, but which English biographies have stood the test of time, apart from Boswell's *Johnson*? 'Definitive' is not an adjective to be trusted; 'ephemeral' is a truer definition of the biographical genre. I would suggest that Gibbon's view squashes Strachey flat: 'A cloud of critics, of compilers, of commentators, darkened the face of learning; and the decline of genius was soon followed by the corruption of taste.'

Strachey did not participate in the 1914 war, whether because he was as unfit as he looks in photographs or because he was a conscientious objector. While the fighting was at its fiercest and the lists of casualties lengthened, he wrote an account of his apparently unrequited passion for his postman – the late John Wells, actor, teacher, humorist, recited it in mincing accents as a party piece. In Strachey's more serious work he was a debunker, puncturing reputations, and was thought by his contemporaries to be opening a window on the corridors of power and allowing the draught to blow away the dust. But who reads his biographical studies now? They remind me of the clever weakling at school who blows raspberries at the bloods from a safe distance.

The art of writing is not necessarily 'delicate' in my opinion, and I would require a definition of 'humane' before I could agree with that epithet. Shakespeare was not merely 'delicate', nor was he 'humane' in any sense. He was a creative writer, the leader of the pack of the recreators of reality, the seminal poets, the novelists fashioning new worlds instead of picking old ones to pieces.

But alas, here in the land of Shakespeare and co., Strachey's claim that he was doing the right thing and the imaginative writers were wrong has been influential. There have been too many literary critics who dared not review fiction in case they were mistook, failed to spot a winner, tipped also-rans, made fools of themselves and ruined their reputations as know-alls. The consequence is that high literary art has languished in my lifetime. Readers are not guided towards better books, they stick to biographies which neither strain nor endanger. Commercial interests as usual follow rather than lead public opinion, and therefore shun the best of everything; publishing houses have started to shut out fiction, which is our national literary glory; gifted writers can seldom afford to write the books that virtually no publisher will look at; and in the twilit field of literature the Philistines stand with their flat feet on the necks of the beautiful beasts they have slaughtered.

26 January

Philistia is another world, and its denizens speak only a limited pidgin version of our language. If you talk to them of creative writers, they think you mean productive ones. If you refer to imaginative writing, they point at inventive books by Jules Verne or Ian Fleming. Their idea of the recreation of reality is Coronation Street, and the only difference they see between Coronation Street and *War and Peace* is that the latter is foreign and takes a long time to read. For them the written word spells trouble compared with films and TV; and the only good read is the book of the film. The adjectives 'distinguished, sensitive, moving, intricate, subtle, unique' put them right off the reading matter they are applied to.

In Philistia, as in every other expression of life on earth, vegetable, animal, human, political and social, a class system exists, and it defines reactions to the arts. In the lower depths, 'art' and 'arty' are terms of abuse. As soon as status enters into the picture, 'artistic' is synonymous with a claim to superiority. Then there are families with children doing 'art' at school who live in houses with bookshelves and pictures that are not calendars hanging high on lounge walls. Middle class wives go in for interior decor and trips to London to shop and if possible take in a fashionable exhibition of paintings. Next come the Philistine intelligentsia with their addiction to the novelties that they call 'art'; and the rich, who are proud to pay for the favour and flattery of the clever people, and begin to buy pictures because they are expensive.

On another subject, I cannot for the life of me imagine why many women have now fallen for the theory that they are better off not married to the men they live with and whose children they bear. I can see that dishonest and dishonourable partners and fathers may think they will more easily escape women to whom they are not married; but why do decent sensible men put up with being permanently on approval, and decent women ditto? The perks of being an unmarried or married mother, or a wife or mistress, are nowadays more equivalent – a baby begat out of wedlock is no longer socially disadvantageous, and palimony has become good business. But the propaganda about freedom, that marriage is human bondage whereas love is meant to be a free for all, is drivel and dangerous.

27 January

In my lifetime Adolf Hitler rose from nowhere, conquered an empire, committed suicide, and his empire disappeared. The Soviet Union disintegrated, communist tyrants eventually died, marxism became unfashionable, and all the fellow travellers of the most oppressive political regime in history have been made to look nasty and stupid. The unexpected has shown over and over again that it is bound to happen. Change is inevitable, to coin a phrase. The ultimate value of democracy is that it speeds up the process of change. People, the electorate, people lucky enough to vote in free and fair elections, may not be particularly wise or well-informed, but they are fickle, they change their minds and sack their rulers as soon as possible and for any old reason. Eden began his televised addresses to the nation, 'My friends'; Lord Home had a toothy smile; Macmillan dared to warn the electors that they 'had never had it so good'; Wilson told a half-truth about the 'pound in your pocket'; Heath had a comical laugh; Kinnock was shown on TV falling over in the wavelets of Brighton beach; Margaret Thatcher was a woman; William Hague wore a baseball cap; John Major had connections with circuses; and Tony Blair went to a function in India in a Nehru jacket – it only remains to be seen if Blair is not forgiven for doing so, just as the others were for their offences in the eyes of voters.

29 January

Maybe I should apologise for trying to bear witness to the decline of culture in poor old England. After all, more books are published year on year, more music played, more museums opened, more prizes for 'art' awarded; and every English citizen of every age seems to be either writing a novel, painting a picture, singing in a choir, turning a pot or doing something sculptural. But I stick to my opinion that cultural standards have already gone west or are going south, partly in hopes that the young will contend that I am wrong and prove it.

29 June 2002

I have again hearkened to the call of the wild, that is of fiction, and written *The Stepmother*, a novel inclusive of my idea of another book called *Duress*, instead of attending to my diary. I hope that my final entries will ring down the curtain, switch on the houselights, and send the punters home satisfied and unharrowed.

The best ending of any play or book that I have come across is Armado's little speech at the end of *Love's Labours Lost*: 'The words of Mercury are harsh after the songs of Apollo. You, that way; we, this way.'

The edition of *Roget's Thesaurus* revised and modernised by Robert A. Dutch is the oldest-fashioned and most pedantic of books although it was reissued in 1975. It is a mine of superseded synonyms and a defunct English vocabulary, and I love it. Here are some surprising words listed under the heading 'Darling: favourite, dowsabel, sweetling, chou, mavourneen, pippin, laddie, sonny, fondling, cosset, top seed, top liner, honeypot.'

2 July

Misuse of the English language: alarmed car, leather described as 'piggy calf', and a dog as a 'pedigree mongrel'. These are two examples of politically correct fibs: 'vegetarian dragon', and 'Baa Baa, rainbow sheep'.

I cannot help wondering if butterflies were meant to be called flutterbys – flutterbys is more descriptive, and butter is nothing to do with the insect. Mistakes are often made, believe it or not. The first Duke of Devonshire is supposed to have wished to be called the Duke of Derbyshire, but wrote so illegibly that he was awarded a county where he had no interests.

The following quotation from *Adolphe* by Benjamin Constant is more useful than comment on politics: 'What surprises me is not that man needs a religion, but rather that he should ever think himself strong enough or sufficiently secure from trouble to dare to reject any one of them. I think he ought, in his weakness, to call upon them all.'

4 July

A man on the London to Brighton train was overheard speaking on a mobile phone probably to his wife thus: 'It's me, dear ... Okay, thanks - yourself? ... That's good ... A bit long and boring, but we're in the outskirts of Liverpool now ... Just for the night, dear – I'll be back tomorrow ... Oh, I'll find somewhere to stay – my business contacts will have arranged accommodation, I daresay ... No, sweetie, sorry, I won't have time to ring today, not with all the meetings that are planned ... Well, I'll ring you tomorrow morning to let you know when I'll be home ... Same here, my dear ... Bye-bye, sleep well!'

We have recently had an old lavatory replaced by a new one. The latter bears as trademark on its pan the word Bloomsbury. To use it is a form of literary criticism.

5 July

On the white wall of a humble out-of-the-way church in France there is a small marble plaque bearing this touching legend: *Merci* 1915–1918.

Another wall in France was defaced with the sprayed rallying cry '*A mort les ar...*' If the graffiti merchant had not been interrupted, would he or she have completed the last word thus, '*armes*' or '*armées*' or even, nostalgically, '*aristos*'? As it was, a wit had added two unexpected letters in oil paint, 'ts' – 'Death to the arts!'

6 July

The first rule of craftsmanship, literary composition included, is to carry on as if time were unlimited. You aim to get the thing right however long it takes – deadlines are of secondary importance, ideally even money should not be allowed to exert its baneful influence. Perfection is unattainable, they say, but rightness can and must at least be targeted.

In my seventy-sixth year, after fifty-five years of literary composition, I continue to struggle to curb my impatience, convince myself that I must revise my diary until it is as right as I can make it, and will still have time to write a few more stories, for instance the one already begun, *The Sodbury Crucifix*.

I also promise to remember that no one, no outsider, can help with creative work – yes with polishing it, no with the act of creation or, in a deep sense, with what has been created.

7 July

Dreams wake me almost every morning. They are fraught with anxiety, never carefree. I mourn lost loved ones. I recount my sins of omission and commission. Against my will I remember the twentieth century that I was lucky to survive, and that it could all happen again. I used to try to describe these dreams to the dedicatee of *The Time Diaries*, but they are as senseless and tedious as surrealist art, and now when I begin to recount one she is apt to say: 'Cut it short!'

She is quite right. Here – again – yet again – I shall follow her advice, bow to my readers and wish them well, and take her out to lunch.

TIME SCALE

22 November 2004

Marking Time was written between 11 June 1999 and 31 January 2000. *Extra Time* was written between 1 January 2001 and 7 July 2002.

My three short novels, *The Third Time*, *The First Nail* and *The Last Straw*, were written during the writing of *The Time Diaries*, and published as *Tales of Love and War* by The Book Guild of Lewes.

The Book Guild has also published *Byron's Diary* and *The Stepmother* in the year 2003, and *The Sodbury Crucifix* and *Damnation* in 2004.

Games of Chance, finished in November 2003, is ready for publication in February 2005, and *The Time Diaries* in the autumn of 2005. And I dare to hope that *According to Robin* and *Odd Woman Out* will be published in 2006.

Further books beckon me, 'in my dreams', as today's jargon would put it: *The Poor Rich*, a novel, *Harlequinade*, a selection of the books in the Harlequin Edition, and *The Best of Three*, a reissue of my selection of items from my three books of short stories.

The Time Diaries began by being my answer to retirement. Having publicly stated that I would write no more fiction, I had either to write something else, for instance a diary, or give up the ghost. So I became a diarist, but temporarily. Fate begged to differ, as proved by the paragraphs above. They, those paragraphs, not only advertise my wares, but also, since I have been prolific against my expectations and despite my age, re-emphasise the explicit and implicit message of all my books, which is: you never know.

INDEX

Acton, Sir Harold, 160–2
Allen, Walter, 122
Altrincham, Lord, 188
Altrincham, Lady, 188
Amis, Kingsley, 103
An-tAthair-Síoraí, Adam, 175
Ardito, Carlo, 10, 134
Asquith, Lady Cynthia, 142, 154
Asquith, Simon, 142
Ayer, Sir Alfred, 54

Bardsley, Lady Rose (sister of JF), 60
Baudelaire, Charles, 148
Beaton, Cecil, 169
Beaufort, Duke of, (David), 15
Beckett, Sir Martyn, 157
Beevor, Anthony, 43
Beevor, Artemis, 49
Bellow, Saul, 29
Bence-Jones, Mark, 37
Berlin, Sir Isaiah, 109
Bernhardt, Sarah, 156
Betjeman, Sir John, 141–2, 144, 187
Bin Laden, Osama, 179, 181

Biss, Carol, 94
Blacker, Dr Thetis, 157
Blair, Cherie, 62
Blair, Tony, 51, 62, 168, 179, 191, 192–3, 201
Boswell, James, 10, 197
Bradbury, Malcolm, 79, 107
Brecht, Bertolt, 156
Brewer, Professor Derek, 113–14
Brice, Vera, 55, 69, 77, 88, 123
Bridgeman, Viscountess, (Harriet), 15
Brittain, Judy, 24
Britten, Benjamin, 132
Brontë, Charlotte, 189
Brophy, Bridget, 193
Brown, Sally, 70
Bury, John, 132
Byron, Lord, 127, 172

Capel, Anne, *see* Higgins
Capel, Arthur, 6
Capel, June, *see* Hutchinson
Carron, Dr Helen, 114, 117
Cary, Joyce, 109
Cavendish, Lady Elizabeth, 187

Cecil, Lord David, 109, 153, 161
Cecil, Jonathan, 22, 40
Cecil, Lady David, (Rachel), 53, 109
Chaplin, Charles, 141
Chateaubriand, Vicomte, 75
Chekhov, Anton, 64
Chilcot, Mr, 195
Cholmondeley, Marquess of, 9
Christie, Audrey, 7
Christie, Gus, 35–6
Christie, John, 7
Christie, Lady, (Mary), 36
Christie, Sir George, 7, 16, 35, 36, 80, 188
Churchill, Sir Winston, 138, 156
Clark, Alan, 37, 56, 106
Clark, Jane, 106
Codrington, Ursula, 8, 156
Colefax, Lady, 147
Connolly, Cyril, 145
Constant, Benjamin, 203
Cooper, Lady Diana, 49, 153–4
Corrigan, Laura, 147
Creston, Dormer, 43
Crook, Diana, 71, 117, 170
Crook, John, 67, 71, 107
Cunard, Lady, 147
Cust, Harry, 49

Dante, 127
David, Elizabeth, 49
Devonshire, Duke of, (Andrew), 15
Devonshire, Duchess of, (Mary), 153
Dewar, Donald, 147
Dickens, Charles, 34, 146
Dostoevsky, Fyodor, 34, 173

Douglas, Lady Patricia, 154
Douglas, Lord Alfred, 154
Douglas-Home, Sir Alec, *see* Home
Douglas-Home, William, 8, 39
Drogheda, Countess of, (Joan), 154
Duffy, Maureen, 193
Dumas, Alexandre, 156
Duncan, I.K., 160
Dunne, Martin, 37
Dunne, Alicia, (Mish), 37
Dutch, Robert A., 202

Eden, Countess of Avon, (Clarissa), 139
Eden, Earl of Avon, (Anthony), 138–9, 201
Eden, Sir Timothy, 139
Eden, Sir William, 139
Edward VIII, 15
Edwards, Oliver, 10
Egremont, Lord, 15
Einstein, Albert, 141
Eliot, T.S., 109, 144–5
Elizabeth II, Queen, 76, 168

Fane, Gillian (wife of JF), 6, 7, 18, 24, 25, 28, 37, 40, 66, 67, 70, 80, 98–9, 106, 150–1, 176, 185–7, 196
Fane, Harry (nephew of JF), 126
Fitzgerald, F. Scott, 112–13, 116
Fitzgerald, Zelda, 113
Fleming, Anne, 140
Fleming, Ian, 124, 140, 156, 199
Forster, E.M., 146
Frost, Sir David, 11

G, *see* Fane, Gillian
Gaitskell, Hugh, 140
Garbo, Greta, 170
George V, 14
George VI, 9, 14
Gibbon, Edward, 181, 197
Gibson, Lady, (Dione), 17
Gibson, Lord, (Pat), 16
Gide, André, 134
Gladwyn, Lord, 94–5
Glazebrook, Ben, 13, 17, 19, 30, 47–9, 52–3, 57–8, 60–1, 66, 72, 87, 90, 123
Glazebrook, Sara, 53
Goering, Emmy, 21
Goethe, Johann Wolfgang von, 127
Gogol, Nikolay, 192, 194
Goldwyn, Sam, 131
Green, Henry, 94
Green, Maurice, 33–4
Grigg, Sir Edward (Ned), *see* Altrincham
Grigg, Joan, *see* Altrincham
Grigg, John, 5, 10, 15, 157, 163, 184, 188–91
Grigg, Patsy, 5, 6, 93, 163, 191

Hague, William, 201
Hall, James, 132
Hall, Sir Peter, 132
Hamilton, Patrick, 113
Handel, George Frederick, 7
Hardy, Thomas, 34
Hartley, L.P., 109, 141, 156
Hatwell, Michael, 134
Hayward, John, 145
Hazlitt, William, 75
Heath, Sir Edward, 201
Helen of Troy, 158
Hemingway, Ernest, 116

Higgins, Anne (half-sister of JF), 6, 20, 21, 28, 49, 110, 124
Higgins, Peter, 49, 124
Hitler, Adolf, 51, 92, 95, 201
Home, Lord, 201
Howard, Brian, 32
Huddleston, Miles, 31
Hutchence, Michael, 30
Hutchinson, Lord, (Jeremy), 6, 78
Hutchinson, Lady, (June), (half-sister of JF), 5–6, 20, 22, 28, 78, 170, 188
Huxley, Aldous, 147

Islington, Lady, (Anne), 188, 191

Jackson, Charles, 113
Janacek, Laos, 162
Jarman, David, 177
Jay, Lady, 38
Jay, Peter, 38
Jebb, Miles, *see* Gladwyn
John, Augustus, 102
John, Gwen, 102
Johnson, Dr Samuel, 10, 50
Jones, David, 109

Keats, John, 127, 131
Kinnock, Neil, 201
Koestler, Arthur, 23, 96
Kout, Jiri, 35

Lawrence, D.H., 146
Lawrence, Frieda, 146
le Vot, André, 112
Lees-Milne, Alvilde, 106, 170
Lees-Milne, James, 61, 106, 170
Leeson, Nick, 10, 54

Lehnhoff, Nikolaus, 35
Lenin, 19, 108
Lewis, Rosa, 139
Liszt, Franz, 16
Lloyd-Webber, Lord, 145
Lovat, Lady, (Laura), 126, 154
Lowry, Malcolm, 113

McCarthy, Helen, 36
Macmillan, Harold, *see* Stockton
Madonna, 176
Major, John, 201
Mann, Thomas, 141
Marin, Minette, 119
Marsh, Sir Edward, 156
Marx, Karl, 18, 19, 95
Mary of Teck, Princess, 14
May, Val, 67
Michelangelo, 182
Montherlant, Henri de, 120
Moore, Joan, *see* Drogheda
Morrell, Lady Ottoline, 53, 146–7
Murdoch, Iris, 54
Murray, John, (Jock), 62, 72, 144

Nabokov, Vladimir, 192
Napoleon, 108
Nicolson, Ben, 142
Nicolson, Sir Harold, 43, 141–2, 143, 170
Nissen, George, 94–5
Nissen, Jane, 94–5
Nitescu, Adina, 15, 16
Noel, Gerard, 169, 175
Norwich, Viscount, (John Julius), 49
Nureyev, Rudolf, 52

Origo, Iris, 197

Orwell, George, 127
Osborn, Christopher, 6, 78
Osborn, Franz, 6, 96
Osborne, John, 106
Oxford, Countess of, (Margot), 64

Payne, Ann, 70
Pearson, Robin, 39
Petropoulos, Jonathan, 176
Picasso, Marina, 23
Picasso, Pablo, 24
Pinter, Harold, 174
Plato, 11
Plomer, William, 156
Pope-Hennessy, Dame Una, 144
Pope-Hennessy, James, 143–4
Pope-Hennessy, John, 143
Powell, Anthony, 161–2
Proffitt, Stuart, 69
Prokofiev, Sergey, 52
Proust, Marcel, 89, 109, 131, 146, 182
Pushkin, Alexander, 127, 182

Q (Sir Arthur Quiller-Couch), 31
Quennell, Peter, 120

Rattle, Sir Simon, 131
Recamier, Mme, 75
Ribblesdale, Lord, 126, 139
Robinson, Leslie, 48, 88, 123
Robinson, Nick, 57, 61, 66, 87
Rosenbaum, Ron, 95
Ross, Alan, 105–6
Rowling, J.K., 186–7
Russell, Bertrand, 53

Sackville-West, Vita, 141–2, 143, 153–4, 170

St John, Lord, (Norman St John Stevas), 114
Sargent, John, 126
Sassoon, Siegfried, 127
Schiff, Sydney, 194–5
Schiff, Violet, 128, 144, 195
Scott, Sir Walter, 124, 127
Seago, Edward, 100–2
Seago, John, 100
Shakespeare, William, 52, 64, 102, 198
Shaw, Bernard, 68
Sheldon, W.H., 181
Shelley, Percy Bysshe, 127
Shephard, Tony, 9, 176
Short, Eileen, 97
Sinclair-Stevenson, Christopher, 62
Sitwell, Edith, 146
Sitwell, Sir Osbert, 127, 146
Sitwell, Sir Sacheverell, 127, 146
Smetana, Bedrich, 25
Smiley, Lavinia, 17
Snow, C.P., Lord Snow, 103, 109
Solzhenitsyn, Alexander, 182
Spalding, P., Anthony, 109
Stalin, 51, 108
Steiner, George, 95
Stern, James, 31–2
Stern, Tanya, 32
Stockton, Earl of, 139–40, 201
Stoppard, Sir Tom, 137
Strachey, Lytton, 197–8
Swire, Sir Adrian, 99
Swire, Gillian, *see* Gillian Fane
Swire, Jock, 196
Swire, Juliet, 196

Thatcher, Sir Denis, 140

Thatcher, Lady, 140, 187, 201
Tolstoy, Leo, 8, 34, 58, 64, 125, 127, 172–3, 182
Tomkins, Richard, 31, 33
Toynbee, Philip, 141
Tree, Lady Anne, 29, 33, 175
Tree, Michael, 29, 33
Tressler, Dieter, 19–22
Trollope, Anthony, 53
Tudor-Craig, Pamela, 196

Upcott, J.D., 195

van Gogh, 113, 183
Verdi, Giuseppe, 185
Vermeer, Jan, 183
Verne, Jules, 199
Vick, Graham, 71
Victoria, Queen, 9, 92

Warner, Deborah, 131–2
Watkins, A.R.D., 195
Waugh, Auberon, 92–4
Waugh, Evelyn, 24, 93, 141, 161
Waugh, Harriet, 93
Wedgwood, Lady, *see* Tudor-Craig
Welch, Denton, 131
Wells, H.G., 75–6
Wells, John, 198
Westmorland, Earl of, (David), (brother of J.F.), 60, 174, 188
Westmorland, Countess of, (Diana), (mother of J.F.), 153, 188
Wilde, Oscar, 68, 154–5
Wilkinson, Patrick, 146, 195
Williams, Dorian, 195

Williams, Tennessee, 113
Wilson, Lady, (Barbara), 126
Wilson, Sir Harold, 201
Windsor, Duchess of, 15
Windsor, Duke of, 15
Wodehouse, P.G., 13
Woodforde, Parson, 56

Wrench, Janet, 138
Wyatt, Lord, (Woodrow), 49–50, 56
Wyndham, John, *see* Egremont
Wyse, John, 195

Yates, Paula, 30